FAMOUS
TENNIS PLAYERS

FAMOUS
TENNIS PLAYERS

by Trent Frayne

ILLUSTRATED WITH PHOTOGRAPHS

Dodd, Mead & Company · *New York*

Copyright © 1977 by Trent Frayne
All rights reserved
No part of this book may be reproduced in any form
without permission in writing from the publisher
Printed in the United States of America

1   2   3   4   5   6   7   8   9   10

Library of Congress Cataloging in Publication Data

Frayne, Trent.
    Famous tennis players.

    Includes index.
    1. Tennis players—Biography.   I. Title.
GV994.A1F7   796.34'2'0922   [B]   77-6501
ISBN 0-396-07470-7

To June, naturally

CONTENTS

FAMOUS
TENNIS PLAYERS

Bill Tilden

BIG BILL TILDEN

[1893–1953]

O<small>N THIS MARROW-CHILLING DAY</small>, this day when the frigid winds off Lake Michigan are whipping the awnings of the Skokie Country Club in Glencoe, an upset of tall proportions is in the making in the final of the Illinois state tennis championships.

William Tatem Tilden II, the national singles champion for the past five years, is down 5–2 in the fifth set, and Howard Kinsey, the fourth-ranked player in the country, has him on the run, the winner of five straight games in this decisive set.

Five thousand spectators sit chilled and huddled, pressing blankets closer around their knees, hunching their shoulders against the icy winds, warmed only by the knowledge they are witness to a rare and startling moment.

All eyes are on Tilden as the players change ends. He looks gaunt and weary, the broad shoulders bent, the stride in the long lean legs slow and listless. He pauses by a table near the umpire's chair on which sits a pitcher of ice water, untouched by the two men on this overcast and dismal day. Suddenly, he straightens. Quickly, he pulls off the white V-necked sweater he's worn all afternoon. Now he grasps the pitcher, lifts it high above his head and, with a quick turn of his hands, whirls the water and the chunks of ice in a long drenching cascade on his head and shoulders. He lifts a towel from the table, nonchalantly dabs it against his forehead and chin, and carefully dries his hands. Then, as the crowd cries out in startled laughter and surprise, he walks briskly to the baseline and calls for the balls to serve. He rattles off four straight games, loses one as the shaken Kinsey strives to regain his composure, and then runs off two more games to wrap up the match.

Big Bill Tilden, who died at sixty in 1953, was a man whose name became a synonym for the game he played, partly because of the flamboyant and often bizarre nature of his personality and many of his triumphs. A well-to-do and paradoxical Philadelphian, he dominated the courts of the world through the first half of the 1920s and his name was still reverberating across them fifty years later when tennis rushed to unprecedented heights of popularity.

Tilden won seven United States national championships, six in a row from 1920 through 1925 and the last in 1929. He won the Wimbledon title in 1920, 1921, and 1930 and played on the American Davis Cup team eleven years, leading the battle that kept the trophy in the U.S. for seven straight years at a moment in history when the international matches carried towering nationalistic overtones.

Except for the emergence of the famed French Musketeers—Henri Cochet, René Lacoste, Jean Borotra, and Jacques Brugnon—in the mid-1920s Tilden might easily have been the world's most successful player for the en-tire decade. As it was, he came very close to being just that and, as Lacoste wrote in his memoirs, "It took all of us to contain the great Tilden, not just any one of us."

Tilden's name continued to be the yardstick against which new stars were measured long past the 1920s and in the first half of the century no one came close—at least in the United States. In December 1949 when national polls were determining the names of the top players of the half century in all sports, Tilden was voted as the greatest in his game by a margin larger than that gained by any player in any of the major sports. For years, the words Tilden and tennis belonged together.

Big Bill. That was his sobriquet, although it was some-what misleading. Because of his bone structure—wide shoulders, very narrow hips, skinny legs—he appeared to be six-feet-three or four as he stretched his long frame to deliver an overhead smash. In truth, he was six-feet-one and weighed only 155, flat of stomach, sharp featured, and gangling.

He became a singular figure as much for the flair and melodrama he brought to the courts as for the dimension of many of his victories. It was the conviction of Allison Danzig, who travelled the tennis trail for the *New York Times* for nearly half a century, that the court on which Tilden romped was his stage, that he loved to posture on it, and that he played to the crowds from it, often toying with them deliberately. "To win the crowds to his side, he went to lengths that seemed to border on lunacy," Danzig wrote. "He would allow his opponent to gain so big a lead as to make his own defeat appear inevitable. Then, from this precarious position, he would launch a spectacular comeback that had the crowd cheering him and that invariably ended with an ovation from the stands when he won."

In many of his high moments Tilden was not content simply to win; he seemed compelled to win dramatically, sometimes even with a gauche gusto as on the day in 1925 in the Illinois state final when he left poor Kinsey bewildered. Indeed, bewilderment was an emotion experienced by many a Tilden rival. Often, just when it appeared that Tilden was ready for wrapping, he would suddenly lift his game to remarkable peaks and the opponent would be left with not just defeat but the nagging notion that Tilden had let him get far ahead so that the overtaking would be more fun.

Tilden made a particular foil of the American whom he succeeded as the country's No. 1 player, William (Little Bill) Johnston, a crowd favorite wherever he played, a player once described by the French master René Lacoste as "the most ideal of sportsmen." In 1919 Johnston beat Tilden in the U.S. national finals, and forever thereafter Tilden lashed and often humiliated him. In 1920 Tilden won in five sets at Wimbledon, and the consensus was that he'd done it only because of his superior serve. So in the 1921 U.S. nationals he beat Johnston again in five sets without ever calling on his powerful cannonball, merely putting the ball in play and then trading baseline shots and outsteadying Johnston. Johnston was exhausted at the end.

A year later on the same center court Johnston raced to a two-set lead. Tilden won the next, but then Johnston broke his service twice to get a 3–0 lead in the fourth. As the players changed ends an official chided Tilden that

Little Bill finally was showing the player's real merit. Tilden ripped off six straight games to win that fourth set, and was almost as formidable in the clincher. Johnston supporters still were convinced their man was the best, noting that Tilden's better physical proportions and greater stamina in the long match had been the difference this time. So Tilden fixed *that* two years later. Johnston had reached the Forest Hills final without losing a set, so obviously he was at the top of his game, physically and mentally. Tilden cut him down 6–1, 9–7, 6–2, and it became evident to the shattered Johnston and his silenced coterie that Big Bill could beat Little Bill anytime, anywhere, under any conditions.

If Tilden had been simply flamboyant in some of his cliff-hanging triumphs, most people likely would have forgiven him. But he was also imperious and arrogant. "He was a supreme egoist," Allison Danzig wrote. "Opinionated and temperamental." Al Laney, who covered tennis for years in the old *Herald-Tribune,* called him "quarrelsome and unreasonable, very hard to get along with." George Lott, an outstanding doubles player in Tilden's time, said that when Big Bill entered a room he took over and, worse, that he *expected* to take over. "It was as though you were in the presence of royalty," Lott said. Tilden was the sort of man who never felt he was wrong—about anything.

Apart from tennis, Tilden centered his life around bridge and the theatre. Once, when he came into an inheritance of $30,000 he used the money to produce *Dracula* on Broadway with himself in the title role, and it was a disaster. He tried writing, too—droopy novels usually inveighing against the evils of alcohol, which he personally abhorred. He also could not abide soft drinks. Yet he drank strong steaming black coffee by the potful and chain-smoked cigarettes. He dressed in a slovenly manner and, partly because he disliked disrobing in public, he rarely showered, even after the most gruelling of five-set matches. But he could be an enormously charming man, gracious with people he liked, considerate, and witty. He could not stand stuffed shirts and frequently clashed with pompous officials of the United States Lawn Tennis Association (USLTA), which was rife with them.

He made one of his most famous stands against the hierarchy of the USLTA during the Davis Cup finals of 1927. The U.S. met France that year, the French anchored as usual by Lacoste and Cochet, the singles stars, and backed by the supreme doubles combination of Borotra and Brugnon.

In the opening singles Little Bill Johnston was handled rather easily by Lacoste, and Tilden pulled America even, crushing Cochet in four sets. Next day, Tilden was slated to partner Frank T. Hunter in the doubles. They had won both Wimbledon and Forest Hills but, for inscrutable reasons, USLTA officials advised Tilden on the morning of the match that Dick Williams would be his partner.

"Splendid," snapped Tilden. "Count me out."

He was advised he was committed to follow instructions.

"Indeed I'm not," Tilden retorted. "I'll be playing bridge in the clubhouse. When you've regained your sanity, come and advise me."

As the morning wore on, blazered officials approached Tilden repeatedly as he played bridge. They ordered, than threatened, then cajoled, finally pleaded with him to change his mind. He would not. Indeed, at one point he rose and, scowling down at them, demanded that they stop interrupting his bridge game. But with the center court surrounded by a sellout crowd, the officials could not maintain their stand. They relented.

"Fine," said Tilden, not raising his eyes from the cards. "I'll dress when we finish this rubber."

Tilden and Hunter won the doubles, all right, but the wily French pair concentrated their shots on Tilden, making him work hard for his points, lobbing to him endlessly and compelling him to jackknife his lean body for energy-draining overheads time upon time. The tactic, of course, was to tire him for Lacoste in their vital singles encounter next day, and it was successful. Recognizing the scheme, Tilden went for an early kill when he engaged Lacoste. But Lacoste played a waiting game keeping the ball in play as best he could while Tilden dominated the first set. Soon Tilden began to weary as the implacable and patient Frenchman kept popping the ball back, and gradually Lacoste gained command.

"The monotonous regularity with which that unsmiling, drab, almost dull man returned the best shots I could hit filled me with a wild desire to throw my racquet at him," Tilden wrote in an autobiography years later. He won only that first set, and the French took the Davis Cup, ending the long American domination when Johnston was unable to handle Cochet in the singles finale.

Tilden, who was 34 in this loss to Lacoste, was a man who arrived late at success. He did not win a major championship until he was 27. At 23 he was ranked 70th in the United States, a virtual unknown. He was 25 when he reached the final at Forest Hills for the first time. By

1920, though, when he was 27, he had arrived as a complete player and he ruled this game with a swashbuckling, dashing, attacking style—a cannonball service that he saved for crucial moments, a flawless forehand, a searing backhand that he developed through tortuous dedication, a blistering overhead, and a firm and deadly volley from either side when he attacked the net. This wasn't often because he was so forceful from the baseline that he seldom needed to rush the net to finish off a rally. But he won five U.S. doubles titles, evidence of his volleying skills, and did so with three different partners, including the redoubtable Vinnie Richards when Richards was a broth of a boy of fifteen. Fifteen tender years.

And, in spurts, Tilden remained an astonishingly able player long past his peak. When he was forty-eight he toured with Donald Budge and was entirely at home trading backhands with the man generally credited with having the most devastating of scoring weapons from that side. When Tilden was fifty he played the defending national singles champion Ted Schroeder and crushed him 6–2, 6–2. Until the day he died ten years later Tilden was capable of short bursts of pulverizing tennis.

It was not until then, in the closing years of Tilden's life, that the public came to know that he was a homosexual. In the late 1940s the glories he had known during his triumphs in the 1920s turned to ashes when newspapers reported two court convictions that resulted in jail terms, one for committing a homosexual act with a minor, the other for violating a parole that directed him not to consort with a minor. He was then in his middle fifties, nearly broke, and frequently handed a stake by old acquaintances; nor was this an era in which America harbored sympathy or understanding for unconventional sexual proclivities in its athletic heroes. Even so, he was playing in occasional pro tournaments and, indeed, was planning to play in Cleveland in June 1953 when he was found dead in his West Coast apartment a half block from Hollywood and Vine. He was lying on his bed, dressed and ready to go out. He had dozed off in this fashion and had died in his sleep. "Just a case of a chap sixty years old who outlived his heart," the coroner said.

Tilden was the youthful survivor of a star-crossed family. His forebears on both sides were British. His mother, Selina Hey, was born in Philadelphia after her father moved there from Yorkshire, England. His father, William Tatem Tilden Sr., was born in Delaware and moved to Philadelphia with his widowed mother. He became successful in the wool-manufacturing business and took Selina Hey as his bride in 1879. Between then and 1883, three children were born to them, two girls and a boy. Then, in a cruel stroke of fate, all three were struck by the highly contagious diphtheria during an epidemic and all died within two weeks, from November 29 to December 12, 1884.

Numbed by the tragedy, the Tildens sadly reordered their lives. William became more deeply involved in business and civic politics. Within a year, they started their family anew when a boy, Herbert, was born and William took a special interest in him. Nearly seven years later, on February, 10, 1893, another child was born, also a boy. Selina named him for her husband, so that in his early years young Bill Tilden was called Junior or June. His father left the boy's rearing to Selina. She adored him, catered to his every want and wish, provided a governess, and pampered him endlessly. He was kept at home and tutored, taught music, and he returned his mother's deep affection. They grew to be the fondest companions.

But when June was fifteen his mother contracted Bright's disease and was confined to a wheelchair. His father by now was considering running as a candidate for mayor of Philadelphia and seldom was home. When Herbert, an undergraduate at the University of Pennsylvania, announced plans to bring home a bride, Junior was sent to Germantown Academy to make room in the house. As a thin angular boy who liked poetry and music, he turned to tennis for an athletic outlet. Later, though he was not interested in broadening his education, he dutifully enrolled at Penn because his father wanted him to study finance. He was a loner whose closest friend was his brother Herbert. Indeed, Herbert really had replaced the young man's busy father in his life, and their relationship was so close that when Herbert's first son was born he named him for his brother, William Tatem Tilden III, thus indicating that Herbert knew Junior would never have children of his own, and was sympathetic.

The three years from eighteen to twenty-one were the worst of young Tilden's life. During his freshman year at Penn in 1912, his beloved mother suffered a stroke, and died. In the summer of 1915 his father was struck by a kidney ailment and, after a brief illness, died suddenly. A few months later Herbert caught a cold during a long afternoon of swimming, and when pneumonia developed he died within five days. Herbert was only twenty-nine. Thus Bill Tilden, at twenty-two, was the only survivor of a family of seven, stricken, shocked, and mourning. He left school and retreated to a room in the home of an aunt, his mother's maiden sister Betsy Hey. Betsy's niece Selina, a woman in her late thirties, lived with her and looked after her and now, with her grieving cousin in the house, she turned her attention to him, too.

This woman, who carried the same name Tilden's mother had known as a girl, understandably had an enormous effect on the life of this shattered young man. She comforted him, spent long hours talking with him, slowly and patiently impressing upon him that he couldn't spend his life in melancholy privacy. She encouraged him to return to tennis, to find release in the exhilaration of the game. And he did. He turned so wholeheartedly to it that within five years he became the world's ranking player.

He had been a good tennis player, though far from a dedicated one, during his years at Penn, relying on his big service and strong forehand. These instruments served him well enough in the first couple of years of his new dedication to the game, but soon he was meeting players far too skillful to be intimidated by these lonely weapons. He was knocked out of his first Forest Hills tournament in 1916 in the first round. But a mere two years later he had added a defensive backhand stroke that served him adequately enough to enable him to reach the final. He lost, and lost again a year later in his first meeting with Little Bill Johnston. Johnston was clever enough to keep the ball away from Tilden's strength on key points and into his weaker backhand area.

"It was Johnston's ability to pound my backhand stroke to a pulp that taught me I had to have an offensive shot there," Tilden wrote later. "The following winter I worked indoors four days a week on my backhand with a friend at Providence, Rhode Island. I hit so many that I was beginning to see them in my sleep, and by the time we went to England for the 1920 Davis Cup matches I had finally added an offensive backhand."

And so, in the summer of 1920, Tilden emerged at the top rank of the world's players when he became the first American to win the singles championship at Wimbledon, a tall, gaunt, dashing figure, broad shouldered and lean as a whippet. "No other player could hit with such pace and control from both sides," Allison Danzig wrote in *The Times* upon reflection years later. "Donald Budge's backhand is usually rated ahead of all others, but not by those who saw Tilden in his prime."

It was in that 1920 Wimbledon final that Tilden first revealed his propensity for the unusual. He opposed the defending champion, Australia's Gerald Patterson, the world's No. 1 player who had a good all-round repertoire except for an unusual corkscrew backhand, his weakest weapon. Usually, players hopeful of handling Patterson attacked that part of his game, but not Tilden. The American opened by directing almost all of his shots at Patterson's strength, his forceful and dependable forehand, and the Australian quickly assumed a 4–0 lead.

Slowly, though, Tilden caught up to Patterson's pace, and the final four games of the set were divided equally as Patterson emerged with a 6–2 jump. As the players changed court for the start of the second set Tilden caught the eye of a friend in the gallery. He smiled and nodded slowly. As the match wore along, the friend became aware of the significance of that smile: Tilden had pulled his game to equal terms with Patterson's strong forehand and the champion had nowhere to turn. His backhand was no match for Tilden's shots and his forehand was unable to penetrate Tilden's defense. Tilden ran off with three straight sets.

Tilden nailed down his domination of the international tennis scene that year by leading America to the Davis Cup, the first of seven straight triumphs, and by winning his first U.S. national championship in five sets with Billy Johnston. In the last half of the decade of the 1920s Tilden engaged in numerous classic matches with the French Musketeers, particularly with Cochet and Lacoste, and in 1928 an international incident was created by USLTA officials, who by then despised Tilden's cavalier attitude toward them, in the Davis Cup challenge round between the U.S. and France.

Tilden was then thirty-five, perceptibly slower though no less forceful, and so the French were slight favorites to retain the trophy on home ground. In these circumstances, the USLTA reasoned the time was ripe to rap Tilden's knuckles: They announced his suspension from amateur tennis in a belated decision relating to his practice of writing tennis articles for various syndicates whenever he was engaged in a major tournament. He had been doing it for years but officialdom had chosen to look the other way as long as he had been winning. But now that Cochet and Lacoste, and the doubles stars Borotra and Brugnon, seemed to have the Cup safely in hand, the officials were ready for another attack on their prickly tormentor. Tilden was suspended for six months for accepting money for his writings, specifically those during the recent Wimbledon championships.

But what the USLTA hadn't bargained for was Tilden's immense popularity in France. All seats at the Stade Roland Garros in Paris were sold for the Davis Cup matches and when the suspension was announced a cry went up that was heard clear across the Atlantic. Tilden was pictured as an international martyr and, in the end, the American ambassador in Paris, Myron T. Herrick, intervened on Tilden's behalf, apparently at the behest of President Calvin Coolidge, and reached an arrangement with the USLTA whereby Tilden's suspension would be delayed until after the Cup matches.

Delighted by this turn of events, Tilden rushed to the court to practice for his opening round match with Lacoste, who had beaten him four straight times over the previous two years. His game wasn't sharp in a long practice session, nor was it under control in the first set against Lacoste, who won easily, 6–1. But then Tilden abandoned his smashing style and turned to a patient retrieving game of chops and lobs and slices that jarred the Frenchman's timing and finally threw him off his game entirely. Tilden won in five sets and Lacoste was dumbfounded.

"Two years ago I learned at last how to beat that man," he said in disbelief afterwards. "Now, on my home court, he beats me. I never knew how the ball would come off his racquet, he concealed it so. I had to wait to see how much it was spinning, and sometimes it didn't spin at all. Is he not the greatest player of them all?"

France repeated its Davis Cup victory, however, sweeping the next four matches, including Cochet over Tilden in the concluding singles match. But, next year, Tilden was back on top again. He won at Forest Hills for his seventh U.S. national championship, and climbed over everyone a year later at Wimbledon. By then he was thirty-seven. During the following year, in 1931, he turned professional, launching the Tilden Tennis Tour in which he was the star attraction, and in later years he was joined by Cochet, Ellsworth Vines, and the British star Fred Perry. Although these were the years of the Depression, the enterprise was profitable and people flocked to see the fabled Big Bill.

In the early 1930s Tilden became the darling of the movie crowd in Hollywood. Clifton Webb rented Constance Bennett's estate one summer and brought in Tilden to coach the stars—Greta Garbo, Katharine Hepburn, Tallulah Bankhead. Tilden became friendly with Charlie Chaplin and Chaplin frequently arranged tennis parties at which Bill partnered and taught other film celebrities—Errol Flynn, Joseph Cotten, Montgomery Clift, Spencer Tracy, and Olivia deHavilland.

But almost all of his acquaintances turned on him when the stories of his homosexuality broke in the newspapers and even his oldest friends snubbed him at Forest Hills, some literally turning their backs on him. His name was stricken from the alumni files at Penn, his pictures removed from the walls of the Germantown Cricket Club where he'd scored many of his Davis Cup triumphs. To this day, there is only one picture of him—a wire-service snap—mixed among those of numerous other champions in the men's locker room at Forest Hills.

Hardly anyone turned out for his funeral in Los Angeles. After it, his remains were cremated and shipped to Philadelphia and buried beside the graves of his parents and his brothers and sisters at Ivy Hill. A single inexpensive stone marks the burial place. In a sad summing up of the triumphs and tragedy of William Tatem Tilden II, no one has said it better than Frank Deford who referred to that small stone tablet in his biography of Tilden published twenty-three years after Big Bill's death: "It is the only monument of any kind anywhere in the world—at Forest Hills, Wimbledon, Germantown, anywhere—that pays tribute to the greatest tennis player who ever lived."

THE FRENCH MUSKETEERS

[1927–1932]

FOR ONE BRIEF AND BRILLIANT MOMENT, France produced the finest national team in tennis history, ruled most of the world's courts for six straight years from 1927 through 1932, and then sank permanently back into the anonymity it had sprung from, defying rational understanding.

Often, one singles player is dominant enough to inspire a country's Davis Cup eminence—Tilden for the U.S. in the early 1920s, Budge and Kramer in later years; Fred Perry for Britain in the mid-1930s; Sedgman, Hoad, and Laver for the Australians in the 1950s and 1960s; and, most recently, Bjorn Borg for Sweden in the mid-1970s. But France, before and after its hot streak, had nobody worth an international franc and yet somehow came up with *four* in its one spectacular splurge.

Three of them, Henri Cochet, René Lacoste, and Jean Borotra, ganged up on Big Bill Tilden to deprive him of complete domination of the decade of the 1920s, and were Davis Cup champions for those six uninterrupted years. Inevitably, these high-flying Frenchmen were called the Four Musketeers.

Borotra, famed as the Bounding Basque, won at Wimbledon in 1924 and repeated in 1926. Lacoste, an aristo-

Jean Borotra

Henri Cochet

René Lacoste

cratic millionaire, won there in 1925 and 1928. Cochet, an imperturbable sphinx who had been a ballboy, was the titleholder in 1927 and 1929. For his part, Brugnon was one of the all-time great doubles players who won Wimbledon's doubles championship four times, a record. He did it twice with Cochet, in 1926 and 1928, and twice with Borotra, in 1932 and 1933. In addition, in their limited appearances at Forest Hills, the French pair of Cochet and Lacoste won three American singles championships, Lacoste in 1926 and 1927 and Cochet in 1928.

For whatever reason, the Musketeers were unique. Before them, only A. H. Gobert, a World War I pilot, and W. H. Laurentz, a Belgian who won the world's hardcourt championship in 1920, were known beyond the borders of France, and after them their countrymen were of similar inconsequential skills. Only one other Frenchman, Yvon Petra in 1946, ever won at Wimbledon or even came close. Georges Goven, born in 1948, began to confirm his early promise in the early 1970s, twice runner-up in the French Championships and once in the Swedish Open, but his subsequent form was inconsistent and by the mid-1970s he was nowhere. Patrice Proisy, a year younger than Goven, was the runner-up in the French Championships three times, but back and elbow injuries stalled his advance and he, like Goven, faded from view.

This left the Four Musketeers: four players of widely disparate personality and talent who often argued among themselves on the courts, sometimes bitterly, but who always managed to subjugate personal attitudes when the tennis prestige of France was at stake—such as in Davis Cup play or at the world stage of Wimbledon.

Brugnon was the least known of the four for the very good reason that, in tennis, plaudits are reserved for singles stars. Still, Brugnon was the rock upon which the French team prospered in its years of Davis Cup mastery, and it seemed never to matter whom he partnered. Tilden called him "the equal in doubles of anyone who ever lived," and in international competition he was successful with a wide assortment of foreign as well as domestic partners in winning national championships in England, Australia, Germany, and France a total of twelve times. In addition to his four Wimbledon titles, he was runner-up on three other occasions there.

Small, shy diffident, Brugnon was a master of tennis tactics, with a sure instinct for openings and the sort of lightning reflexes that could capitalize on them. His volley was a quick slap of line-hugging accuracy, his best stroke by far from either side. His backhand was not of world class, but he always played the forehand, or right, court where its deficiencies were minimized and when, in his impassive way, he partnered the explosive Borotra, tennis fans witnessed a doubles team of enormous attraction.

Borotra, handsome, extroverted, charming, lived joyfully, a ladies' man and rarely one to say no to a nightcap when the wine was flowing. On court he was flamboyant, too, a man in a dashing black beret bouncing across the lines like the ball he pursued. He was quick, colorful, and confident, with no finesse or delicate touch, just an acrobatic and punishing game, particularly when he volleyed. If he played hard off the court he worked hard on his physical conditioning, too, and his competitiveness drove him many times to victory against superior craftsmen.

Victories over the superbly skillful game of René Lacoste were achievements of determination and endurance, pure and simple.

Because, no question, Lacoste in the late 1920s was equipped with the most classic fundamental strokes in the game, and his analysis of any opponent's strengths and weaknesses became a legend. Whenever he was successful against Tilden—in one period he won four straight matches from him—it was because he refused to probe the great man's "wings"—his forehand and his backhand, both of which could be devastating—but, instead, fed him a variety of drop shots, deep lobs, and went to the net against him only after a forcing shot down the middle, never to the sides. Sometimes, of course, even these tactics could not subdue Big Bill.

Lacoste, austere and phlegmatic, adopted as his symbol the crocodile and had a replica of one embroidered on his tennis shirts (when his career ended he became a manufacturer whose shirts, with their crocodile emblem, were still a quality garment wherever tennis was played in the 1970s). When Lacoste played, the reptile symbolized his determination; after each match anywhere in the world he immediately entered in a notebook his observations of his opponent's game. In 1927 he played his book on Tilden masterfully in the singles final at Forest Hills, changing his game constantly, keeping his shots soft as Tilden rampaged from the service line with his cannonball and with his flashing ground strokes. But Lacoste, swarthy and sleekly blackhaired, inscrutable and unyielding, defended the championship he had won in 1925 in straight sets, 11–9, 6–3, 11–9 in a gruelling match. Tilden had set point three times in the first set, broke Lacoste's service and led 3–1 in the second, and then lost five straight games. He was ahead 5–2 and had two set points in the third but succumbed in a match about which Borotra, who rarely complimented anyone, even a countryman, was to observe: "If René keeps on playing that kind of tennis, how is anyone ever going to beat him?" As it turned out, illness was to remove Lacoste from internatonal play within two years, but it could not eliminate him from the scene.

Indeed, in the mid-1960s Lacoste initiated the most revolutionary change in racquet construction in a century. For years Lacoste had maintained that wooden racquets were outmoded—in the manner of hickory-shafted golf clubs—and that tubular steel was the required element. For years, the tennis establishment and the players regarded his theory as both heresy and lunacy. Eventually, some people in each faction came around when the Wilson Sporting Goods Company bought the rights to Lacoste's brainwave and produced a highly popular (as it turned out) steel racquet called the T 2000.

Of all the Frenchmen—indeed, of all the players of the period—none developed his game to the highest point of efficiency so successfully as Cochet, a smallish, pale, sphinxlike fellow on and off the court, slight and swarthy with black curly hair. "At first sight Mr. Cochet does not appear to be strong," one interviewer recorded in 1928, "but after talking to him a few minutes one realizes that the pinched appearance of his face is due not to unfitness but to strict physical training. His eye is keen and his skin clear. His whole attitude, though reserved and even constrained, speaks of energy, and behind a nervous manner can be sensed the indomitable will power and courage that have brought him through so many memorable battles on the courts."

Allison Danzig, the *New York Times* oracle, once wrote that "Cochet was the greatest natural player the world has seen, with a touch out of this world. He did through sheer genius what Tilden did through years of slavery to the racquet in practicing hours daily, week after week, month after month. Never before has a player come to the courts with so pronounced an instinct for the game, with so gifted a hand for the racquet."

By 1928 Cochet was recognized by most close followers of tennis as the game's best player—he won three victories in the Davis Cup final that year and took both the American and French titles, as well—although it was in 1927 that he pulled off one of the great feats of top-level tennis. At Wimbledon that year he swept to the world's most coveted title by winning his last three matches in five sets after the first two had been won by his opponent. He shaded America's Frank Hunter in the quarterfinals, Tilden in the semis, and then won the championship against his countryman Borotra after the Bounding Basque had reached match point six times.

His comeback against Tilden ranks as one of the most unlikely ever, even against a man who made a career of seemingly impossible victories. The little Frenchman lost the first set 6–2, the second 6–4, and seemed about to be wiped out in the most ruthless fashion in the third. In his book *Covering the Court,* Al Laney of the old *New York Herald-Tribune* wrote that with the beginning of the third set Tilden launched his most devastating attack: "Never on that side of the Atlantic had Tilden struck with such real violence. Cochet searched in vain for an effective weapon to stem the tide as Tilden went steadily on, dominant, domineering and arrogant. It was the Tilden of 1921–1925 back on top, piling up the games. He seemed in a big hurry to get it over with. After banging his way to 5–1 with a cannonball that Cochet could not reach, Bill threw the two balls remaining in his hand over the net behind the service and could hardly wait for Cochet to gather them in and serve what we all thought would be the last game. In the competitors' stand just below the press box I saw Hunter hurrying out to be there when his doubles partner came victorious from the arena. But Frank had still another hour to wait and no congratulations to give at the end of it."

From this point forward it was a different match and no one, not Laney, not Danzig, not anyone writing about it in subsequent years ever was able properly to explain what happened, although no one wanted for a theory. With the score 5–1 and Cochet serving, the players split the first two points. And then, in an astonishing turn of events, Tilden lost *seventeen* consecutive points, something unheard of in top-flight tennis, before or since. Cochet ran off three points from 15–all to win his service and make it 5–2. He broke Tilden at love, won his own serve at love, broke Tilden again at love to level the score at 5–5 and then won two more points on his own service before Tilden broke the string. In the last game of the set, with Tilden serving, Big Bill regained momentary control of the cannonball but, even so, he dropped the deuce game and with it the set, at 7–5. Tilden salvaged flashes of form in the ensuing two sets but never in sufficient stretches to regain the psychological edge, if occasionally the one on the scoreboard. Cochet, volleying with power and accuracy, ran out the match at 6–4 and 6–3.

"I have discussed this match many times with many persons, one of them being Tilden himself," Laney was to write in his book, "and I never have arrived at a satisfactory explanation of what happened, of why the greatest player of all could not win just one more game after the most brilliant play of a long career had taken him to the verge, as we say, of overwhelming victory. He could not win even one single point until it was too late."

Among the theories as to what had gone wrong was Tilden's own that Cochet simply had answered an enormous challenge by lifting his game to the required heights. Also, that Tilden characteristically had let down when he had the match in his grasp so that he could inject his patented dramatics. Also, that the entrance of King Alfonso of Spain into the royal box just as Tilden was on the edge of victory induced him to prolong the match for royalty's entertainment. Whatever it was, it was utterly stunning.

And Cochet wasn't through yet. In the final against Borotra he fell behind by two sets to zero. Scarcely anyone conceded him a chance of successfully completing yet another walk along the tightrope, particularly in light of his emotional and physical trial against Tilden in the semifinal. Once again, though, he began the long road back by levelling the match at two sets all, but then he was down by 5–3 with Borotra serving and leading 40–30, needing only that last point for the Wimbledon championship. In the course of that point, which developed into a marvellous volleying duel in which both players moved into the forecourt to parry and thrust like swordsmen,

Cochet made a shot that, from the stands, seemed to have been struck twice by his racquet, a sort of scoop or double hit. He won the point but the umpire was in doubt and, with Borotra, appealed to Cochet for a decision. He gave it, for himself. He went on to win that game, and the next, to deadlock the match at 5–5, facing match point five more times. Eventually, he prevailed at 7–5.

Cochet was the greatest Frenchman. He won another Wimbledon in 1929 and, with Brugnon, won the doubles there twice and was runner-up twice. He won the French Championships in singles four times (to three for Lacoste) and teamed three times with Brugnon to win the doubles there. In 1928 he was sensational in three Davis Cup wins over the U.S. where Lacoste lost both singles matches to Tilden and Little Bill Johnston but Cochet was able to put down both of them and join with Brugnon to capture the doubles. His victory over Tilden retained the trophy for France.

Cochet was a hard man for Americans to warm to. As his decision indicated in the questionable "double hit" call against Borotra, he was an icy man not given to overt sentimentality. His personality remained largely unknown outside France, partly because he made little effort to learn English (not that he should have, necessarily; but this fact kept him remote from interviewers) and partly because he rebuffed personal questions. The American writer John Tunis once asked him about his early years and the Frenchman's reaction was such that Tunis wrote in *The New Yorker*: "He merely muttered something unintelligible about the ancestry of American reporters."

Cochet was born in Lyon in 1900 and was a ballboy at

the Tennis Club de Lyon where his father was the manager. This presented young Henri with unlimited opportunities to play, and he did whenever he could find an idle member. Since Lyon had two indoor courts in an era when such facilities were scarce, he played year round. The courts had wooden surfaces, supplying true swift bounces that provided the basis of Cochet's later mastery of taking the ball on the rise when receiving service and a skill for bringing off superlative half-volleys during rallies.

As a youth he pounded balls against a wall until he blistered his hand and even in later years whenever his game went off he regained his timing in wall practice. "I believe a beginner should play at least six months against a wall before entering a tennis court," he said once. He developed his footwork by beating the ball against the wall and learned that his best stroking power came with the shoulder pointing to the wall. "In my opinion," he said, "the position of the upper part of the body is more important than that of the feet."

In maturity he was a tiny bundle of sinew, deceptively powerful for a man of five-feet-seven and 130 pounds.

In 1926 as his reputation grew he capitalized on it by opening a tiny shop on a back street in Lyon, selling tennis equipment, and with the burgeoning success of the Four Musketeers he expanded his business operations into a chain of stores, with lavish branches in the Rue d'Antibes at Cannes and the Rue de la Pepiniere in Paris. Luckily for him, his business success did not reflect adversely on his amateur status, as it would have in the U.S. where Tilden came under fire from the USLTA for writing about the game. The French Federation was less stringent about what constituted a breach of amateurism.

By 1933, the dominance of France had disappeared as suddenly as it had arrived. Cochet turned pro, Lacoste was sidelined by illness, and Borotra and Brugnon had passed their peaks. Curiously, the success of the Four Musketeers inspired no successors sufficiently skilled to carry the mantle. In addition, a new star had burst onto the tennis scene in England, the black-haired Briton Fred Perry whose victory over Cochet in the Davis Cup final in 1933 spelled finis for France on the internationsl stage.

FRED PERRY

[1909–   ]

THE CLEAREST PICTURE retained by people who saw Fred Perry at the top of his game is that of a long-striding figure, white clad from shoulder to sole, a swashbuckler bounding toward the net to take a ball on the rise and blistering it with what was quite likely the finest running forehand ever.

If the rest of Perry's game had matched that one devastating shot he'd have been unbeatable. His forehand and Donald Budge's backhand were twin howitzers. Even so, Perry's other strokes were richly adequate to make him a compelling player and, with the running forehand to provide icing for the cake, he achieved a cool pedestal.

Perry reigned the tennis world for four years from 1933 through 1936, and then turned professional and toured first with Ellsworth Vines and later with Budge, successful one-night stands all across the United States and the larger cities of Canada. In 1940 he returned to his native England, comfortably fixed financially, and when World War II ended and tennis returned to the land he became a correspondent for a London newspaper and a television commentator. He occasionally turned up on the American networks during important tour-

Fred Perry

naments in the 1970s when he wasn't performing similar chores for the BBC in England and on the continent. And like the French star René Lacoste, Perry turned successfully to business, and his tennis shirts, with a laurel wreath emblem stitched upon the left breast, still lie attractively alongside those carrying Lacoste's crocodile symbol on merchants' shelves in the 1970s.

Perry won the Wimbledon championship in 1934 and when he repeated in 1935 and again in 1936 he brought off a most unusual feat. Bill Tilden, Budge, Rod Laver, Lew Hoad, and John Newcombe all won back-to-back crowns at the mother temple, but only Perry in modern times turned the trick three years successively. The phrase "in modern times" goes back to the World War I interruption of the classic. Prior to it, a man named A. F. Wilding won four straight years, 1910 through 1913, and before that there were the indomitable brothers Doherty who damned nearly took over Wimbledon and made it their own private playground from 1897 to 1906. They won the men's doubles championship eight times in that ten-year span (they were runners-up on the two other occasions) and they won nine of the ten singles championships. R. F. (Reggie) Doherty won Wimbledon four times in succession during the span that ended in 1900, then lost in 1901 to A. W. Gore. Whereupon H. L. (Laurie) Doherty took over in 1902 and won five straight times.

Once World War I was out of the way, however, Wimbledon became an exceedingly difficult cup of tea for anyone to dominate for long, and in the succeeding sixty years only Perry pulled off a triple. His name is revered not only because of his success there, however. For when he took to the grass at Forest Hills, he really took to it. He won the United States national championship three times, twice in a row in 1933 and 1934 and again in 1936, and he went to Paris with his teammate Henry (Bunny) Austin in 1933 to crack France's domination of Davis Cup competition on the Frenchmen's home turf. Through the next three years Perry and Austin retained the highest of international team awards. Between times, Perry made the endless sea voyage to Australia in 1934 to win that continent's tennis crown at Sydney, and hopped over to Paris to win the French Championship a year later at Stade Roland Garros. In short, over a four-year period, the suave Perry won everything there was to win, and it's hard for a tennis player to do more than that.

Everything he did on the court had flair. His whole game was characterized by quickness of movement during points and between them. He was always on the go, instantly ready to get on with the next point when the last one was finished. If he missed a first serve, the ball was immediately in the air for the second one. Players often requested time from the umpires between Perry's serves not only to slow him down but to give themselves time to adjust to his hurry-hurry style.

Apart from his immaculate appearance, he had the bearing of a self-assured debonair champion, a certain smiling swagger. He had a personal magnetism, a quality that lit up the court; plus black gleaming hair, dark good looks, and a lithe, tall and well-muscled frame. He was equipped, as George Lott observed in *The Fireside Book of Tennis,* with "confidence, concentration, condition, co-ordination, courage and fortitude, determination, stamina, quickness and speed." In truth, apart from those qualities, he didn't have much!

Bad calls rarely bothered Perry. He might give a lines-man an exaggeratedly haughty stare but it was more a play to the gallery than an admonition and he would conclude it with a laugh and get rapidly on with the next point. He was a showman but, before that, he was a competitor who kept himself in year-round top physical condition. When he held a gin-and-tonic there was no gin in the glass; when he affected a pipe, as he almost always did on social occasions, there was no tobacco in it. He played the role of the English gentleman to the hilt.

In the sense that a pip-pip Britisher recognizes a gentleman, however, Perry was not one; not, that is, an old-school-tie, born-to-the-manor gentleman. His father, S. J. Perry, was a man "from trade," meaning he was a businessman. He turned to politics with the socialist Labour Party and was elected to the House of Commons. S. J. dabbled in tennis and his son acquired his introduction to the game by using S. J.'s racquet at the Brentham Garden Suburb Club, and he took to it eagerly. He worked out a compromise arrangement there with school chums dedicated to soccer and cricket. He agreed to play goal for them so they could practice kicking footballs and to bowl for them so they could tune their batting eyes in cricket. They, in turn, fed him returns in tennis so that he could practice his shot-making. Like the French ace Cochet he pounded balls endlessly against a wall to improve the fundamental forehand and backhand strokes.

Perhaps it wasn't merely the appeal of the game itself that attracted Perry. The story is related in most accounts of his career that he had first seen tennis at Devonshire Park in Eastbourne where the South of England championships attracted many of the swells of society each year.

When Perry observed the long lines of expensive automobiles surrounding the club, he asked his father who owned them. "The tennis players," S. J. replied to his fourteen-year-old son. No answer, apparently, could have made a deeper impression on the boy.

One drawback, however, was his continental grip, one which enables all shots—groundstrokes, volleys, service—to be handled without change of grip, an advantage that is usually offset by a lack of power. Since, in the continental, the hand is placed on top of the racquet rather than along its side as in the western grip, it removes the palm of the hand from the side of the handle and limits stability and thrust. Perry, who had a wrist like a tree trunk, overcame the deficiency through sheer strength.

The turning point in Perry's advancement came in the mid-1920s when he reached the doubles final of the Middlesex championships and was seen bursting with energy by a Slazenger company executive, A. R. (Pops) Summers, a tournament official impressed by Perry's speed and quick reactions. Summers believed these twin assets could be converted into success in singles if Perry were to take the ball on the rise. Perry could see the wisdom in the Summers theory and he adopted it readily; indeed, it was merely an extension of his style in Ping-Pong, a game at which he was England's champion, and one in which virtually everyone whacks the ball as it rises from the table.

Hitting a ball this way requires a wrist of champions, and Perry had that, big, tough, and flexible. His forehand was delivered with a buggywhip snap as he worked painstakingly on it, drawing scowls and muttered protests from club members who felt their weekend games were being ruined by the pest blasting balls wildly on a nearby court. Yet Perry persisted—and persisted—and what he developed was a threefold advantage: he saved time reaching the net, belting a rising shot at a not-quite-set opponent; he hustled that opponent and kept him off balance by taking the ball early; he acquired stronger rebound power as the ball skidded low from the grass onto his racquet. Eventually, Perry's opponents recognized that it was more dangerous to run him wide on his forehand than to play the center of the court because with his wrist snap at the moment of impact he could hit a sharp short crosscourt return as easily as he could lace a placement down the line.

His overhead was lethal. He didn't try to overwhelm the ball but placed it cleverly. The spring in his legs matched a basketballer's; getting up high, he could come down on the ball from a tall and deadly angle. And being in great shape he leaped and rushed and bounded as forcefully in the fifth set as in the first.

It took the pooh-bahs of the British Lawn Tennis Association a while to recognize Perry's potential, since most of the members were turned pale by the young man's unorthodox early-ball technique. But when Perry engaged the properly bred Bunny Austin in the British hard-court final in 1930 and held match point on him before yielding and when, two months later, he reached the last 16 at Wimbledon, the dawn began to break and the association dispatched Perry with the British team that toured the U.S., Brazil, Argentina, Chile, and Uruguay. He showed he was on his way by reaching the 16s at Forest Hills and winning the Argentinian Championship.

A year later, to the surprise of most people and the dismay of the Americans, Perry and Austin knocked off a highly favored U.S. team in the round leading to the Davis Cup final against defending champion France. The Americans paid so little heed to the British possibilities that they booked hotel and travel accommodations for Paris. Perry lost on opening day to Francis X. Shields and Austin handled Sidney B. Wood. The American pair won the doubles and appeared well on their way to Paris. But on the third day Perry ran away from Wood, who had beaten him at Wimbledon, and Austin nipped Shields to thwart the American advance on France. The French, however, were not quite ready to yield the trophy they'd retained since breaking the American stranglehold in 1927, though the Challenge Round went right down to the fifth match with the teams locked at two victories apiece. The inscrutable Henri Cochet, calling on all of his experience and guile, handled Perry in that one, 6–4, 1–6, 9–7, 6–3 but, obviously, the British were coming.

Curiously, though, it required another year for them to arrive. Their 1932 campaign was a disaster, Perry's included. He lost to Australian Jack Crawford in the quarterfinal at Wimbledon, and then he and Austin were knocked out of Davis Cup competition by upstart Germany. They had small success in their American tour where Perry realized that the segment of his game being increasingly exploited was his backhand. He set about in the winter of 1932–33 to remedy it and although he improved his port side defensively he was still unable to employ it as an offensive weapon by the time Wimbledon rolled around again and he was unceremoniously sidelined by a brilliant volleying exhibition by South African Norman Farquharson in the second round.

But Perry showed his mettle back at the practice court, spending hour after hour to develop a stroke as short and rapid as his forehand and with the same cocked wrist. In a comparatively brief few months this small neat action was capable of delivering both flat and underspin drives. The magnitude of his progress was underlined when the British rushed past the Americans 4–1 in Davis Cup play and there was no question he had his game at a new peak when he defeated Cochet in the first match of the Challenge Round in Paris. The match was so strenuous that Perry, for the only time in his career, fainted at its conclusion. When Bunny Austin lost to a French newcomer, nineteen-year-old Andre Merlin, the Brits seemed surely doomed because, although illness had removed René Lacoste from competition, the impregnable doubles firm of Borotra and Brugnon was still the world's best. They proved it again in the second day when Perry was kept out of the doubles by his fainting spell and the French had no difficulty with Austin and his new partner, George Patrick Hughes.

A flicker of hope returned when Austin surprised Cochet to tie the round at two matches each on the third day, and then it all came down to Perry and the youngster Merlin, by now, obviously, called The Wizard. Merlin, with little to lose since so little had been expected of him, attacked furiously the moment he was turned loose against the under-the-weather Perry. He won the first set and stormed to set point in the second. But Perry hung in, chasing down every shot, bringing all of his experience into play against this callow youth, and finally carrying it off when Merlin missed an overhead smash at set point in the second. Perry went on to win three sets at 8–6, 6–2, and 7–5 to terminate France's six-year reign and provide Britain with its first Davis Cup victory since 1912.

By now Perry was truly underway. He sailed for America in the early fall to arrive at Forest Hills at a moment in tennis history when every eye was centered on the lithe Australian, Jack Crawford. Crawford had won the Australian Championship for the third time in succession that spring, had mastered the invincible Cochet in the final of the French Championships, had scored a marvellous victory over the richly talented Ellsworth Vines in the Wimbledon final, and now, at Forest Hills, was seeking to close out the Grand Slam.

Crawford by now, however, was over-tensed and over-tennised, and he revealed to the young American Vincent Richards that he just wasn't sure his nerves would stay intact through one more pressurized final. He had struggled through a heat wave in New York that had made tennis difficult and sleep nearly impossible and had managed to reach the final round. There, he was opposed by the resurgent Britisher, Perry. In this emergency, Richards confided to Crawford that, luckily, he happened to have a nerve tonic he was sure would calm the finely drawn Jack.

"What is it, Vinnie? I won't take drugs," Crawford declared.

"No, no, it's not a drug," assured Richards. "It's just a mild tonic you can drop into your tea."

Crawford, who sipped tea during intervals when

48

players changed ends, accepted Richards's offer, and the American laced Crawford's tea with a modicum of—what else?—straight bourbon.

The tonic was slow to produce relief and the tense Crawford dropped the first set 6–3. Then, however, the Richards tonic began to produce a salubrious effect, and the Australian sipped his way to a 13–11 win in the heat and pressure of the second set, and moved ahead with a 6–4 edge in the third.

By then, though, he was either plastered or simply out of shots because Perry rushed through the last two sets at 6–0 and 6–1, the first Brit to win the American crown since Laurie Doherty of the indomitable Dohertys in 1903 and the first foreigner since Cochet five years earlier. Perry's win also ended a two-year run by the towering Ellsworth Vines as America's singles champion.

In a two-month stretch in 1934 Perry did it all. He won Wimbledon, the first Englishman to do so in the quarter century since E. W. Gore's success in 1910, with a complete rout of Crawford in the final. The Australian won only seven points in the second set and although he rallied in the third he was nonetheless swept from the court by 6–3, 6–0, 7–5 in a match in which the American doubles star George Lott later wrote that Perry played the finest tennis of his life, before or since. "It was an awe-inspiring exhibition," said Lott. "I know and I am sure that Fred also knows that on this day he reached the peak of his effectiveness. I see Perry from time to time and we always wind up talking about Fred's Wimbledon. Ordinarily, this would bore me considerably, but it gives me almost as much pleasure to go over the details as it does Fred. I appreciate a champion and on that day I saw one.

Then again, during the reminiscences with Fred, while he recounts his victorious march through the field, I occasionally get a word in to the effect that Lester Stoefen and I won the doubles that year, and I receive a 'Righto' from Fred which increases the enjoyment of the memory."

Three weeks later Perry and Austin retained the Davis Cup against an American challenge in which Perry won the pivotal match over Frank X. Shields in a barn-burner, 6–4, 4–6, 6–2, and 15–13. Perry had match point three times in the marathon before Shields, rushing wildly to the net behind his service, volleyed far out of court and then fell heavily on his stomach and skidded along the turf. Perry threw his racquet twenty feet into the air, leaped the net, and helped Shields to his feet.

At Forest Hills in September Perry retained his American crown, though he very nearly frittered it away in the final against an oncoming Texan, Wilmer Allison. Perry whistled through the first two sets at four and three, then, posturing for the crowd and chasing only the balls he could get easily, he blew the next pair at three and one. He got himself together to lead 5–2 in the fifth set but the grim Texan rallied to hold his service twice and break Perry once to lock it at 5–5. Perry steadied, Allison held for 6–6, and then the Briton ran out the last two.

He seemed on the same route in 1935, knocking off Baron Gottfried von Cramm of Germany in straight sets at Wimbledon, combining with Austin to retain the Davis Cup, 5–0 over the U.S., and sailing through the early rounds at Forest Hills, once more facing Allison when they reached the semifinals. This time, it was a vastly different story. Allison, a marvellous doubles player, utilized his vast skills as a volleyer to run Perry ragged, hitting deep and angling wickedly. Perry stopped play three times in the first set to appeal for quiet from the 14,000 uncommonly noisy spectators. Then, reaching for a deep corner shot in the opening set, Perry fell heavily to the turf. Post-match examination revealed a pulled groin muscle as Perry was overwhelmed 7–5, 6–3, 6–3.

But in 1936 he was back at the top of his game, repeating at Wimbledon over von Cramm in a laugher, 6–1, 6–1, 6–0, and this time it was von Cramm who needed a doctor's assistance. The German had torn a muscle in his leg and asked the referee to apologize to a throng packing every inch of the famous shrine for his poor showing.

By now Perry was an international celebrity, cutting a swath in Hollywood following his marriage to actress Helen Vinson, and entertaining notions of a film career himself or turning professional to tour with Ellsworth Vines in a promotion called Tennis Enterprises run by Francis T. Hunter, Bill Tilden's old doubles partner. In that year of 1936 Daks slacks made him an endorsement offer that reportedly would have amounted to more than a million pounds but he turned it down so that his amateur status would be held intact for Britain's fourth defense of the Davis Cup. But with that accomplished, and with a return to championship form at Forest Hills for his third win there in four years, Perry was ripe for the payoffs of professionalism. He signed with Hunter to tour Canada and the United States for singles matches against Vines, and doubles in which he partnered George Lott against Vines and Tilden.

The tour was undertaken in Madison Square Garden

in 1937. Perry loved the atmosphere, with 18,000 people, many in evening dress and paying up to $9.90 a seat to watch, with linesmen and the umpire in dinner jackets, and with a gross of $51,048. That night, Perry earned $11,000 and Vines $3,400, and the tour went on to attract some $300,000, of which Perry collected $75,000 and Vines a third of that. The players were so evenly matched that it was just a question of whose game was sharper on a particular night. In the end, Vines was the winner, 33 matches to 30, and Perry sailed home to England when the last serve was aced, a man far removed from the fourteen-year-old boy who had admired the long line of shiny automobiles ringing the Devonshire Park tennis courts in Eastbourne.

DON BUDGE

[1915–   ]

THERE ARE THOSE who contend that nobody ever played tennis better than the stringbean California redhead Don Budge, but this is not an easy proposition to be absorbed by people whose only vision of this towering figure is the record book.

Intrinsically, there's nothing *wrong* with Budge's record; all the tall triumphs are plainly etched forever: how he, almost single-handedly, returned the Davis Cup to America in 1937 after its decade in France and England; how he swept a year later to the Grand Slam, the first player ever to win the Australian, French, British, and American national championships in a single year; how he strode in a giant's trappings across the hallowed turf of Wimbledon and Forest Hills, rarely losing a set, much less a match, in two all-conquering years.

But *there's* precisely the rub. Whatever became of the test of time in the case of J. Donald Budge? It's only over the long haul, isn't it, that an athlete's greatness is achieved? What judge can enshrine a man as the best of the best from the evidence of a mere two years?

As it happens, there are at least three judges, each with the credentials of knowledgeability, each of whom was there. First, the New Yorker Sidney B. Wood, who won

Don Budge

Wimbledon in 1931 and was an aging Davis Cupper deposed from the squad four years later to make way for the oncoming twenty-year-old Budge. "When Budge was in his prime no player, past or present, could have beaten him," Wood reflected once, years later. "It was like playing against a concrete wall."

Second, the irrepressible Bobby Riggs who became a mugging ham in the mid-1970s and wrung pounds of promotion out of male chauvinism but who in the youth and prime and seriousness of 1939 succeeded Budge as the world's top amateur at Wimbledon and Forest Hills. "Budge was the most devastating and impressive player I have ever seen," Riggs said once. "Tilden often toyed with his opponents—he would tease them by letting them get close. Ellsworth Vines was inconsistent, a world-beater one day and a patsy the next. Not Budge. He was not only extremely steady, he was explosive. He could blow you off the court."

And, finally, Walter Pate, New York lawyer and tennis buff recruited by the USLTA in 1935 to reconstruct America's Davis Cup fortunes and the man who, as team captain, did precisely that. "I think Budge's Slam rates even above Bobby Jones's in golf," Pate noted. "It's fantastic that a man should be able to go through two years without losing a single match that mattered; one of the great all-time sports achievements."

Budge did everything that could be done to establish a place in the sun and it was no mark against his performance that the men he beat turned out to be of less than lasting stature in the overall picture. By 1937, the British ace Fred Perry had gone on to professional ranks, Jack Crawford had been succeeded as Australia's best by a ris-

ing but still immature Jack Bromwich, and Riggs and
Frank Parker were just emerging in America. That left
the German baron, Gottfried von Cramm, to engage with
Budge for Perry's mantle, and this pair played one match
that historians regard as perhaps the finest ever con-
tested. Still, the baron's main distinction was that he was
probably the best tennis player never to win a major title.
Part of that, of course, was Budge's fault.

Budge's amateur career was foreshortened by his turning professional, and his professional career was curtailed
by the advent of World War II. For three years he dominated the pros as clearly as he'd ruled the amateurs—in
tours in 1939 against Vines and later Perry, in 1940
against Perry, Riggs, and Frank Kovacs, and in 1941, with
no one else left, against the aged though flashily brilliant
Bill Tilden. Then he joined the air force soon after Pearl
Harbor. When he emerged five years later his game was
several notches thinner and, although he was only thirty-
one, he was unable to handle Riggs in a two-month tour,
and that was the end. But when Budge had it, Budge had it,
and that is the picture of him retained by those who insist he
knew no peer.

It may be that he was the most popular champion of all
time—a shy, gangling, jug-eared kid with freckles (what
more compelling combination?). When girls said hello he
blushed in his early years on the eastern amateur circuit;
when his elders complimented him, his normal serious
mien fragmented into a transforming beatific smile. In
his first appearance on the center court at Wimbledon in
1935 Queen Mary arrived during his quarterfinal match
with von Cramm. The crowd in the huge bowl rose and

bared their heads as the monarch was seated and the aristocratic baron stood at the baseline and bowed formally. The ingenuous Budge, never before exposed to royalty, waved and grinned self-consciously. The Queen, recognizing his discomfort, smiled and raised her hand. The crowd responded, too, applauding the defeated Budge indulgently at the end of his match.

Budge's slender physique was deceptive; he was indefatigable and excessively strong. He played with a 16¾-ounce racquet—Tilden's was a full two ounces lighter and so, several decades later, was the one employed by tireless slugger Jimmy Connors. "He let me play with it once," Sidney Wood recalled. "After one set I couldn't hold it anymore; it fell out of my hand. Everything about that man was superhuman."

An oddity about Budge's racquet was that it (or they) carried no leather at the grip. He believed the bare wood was far gentler on the hand, that the leather served no purpose other than to cause blisters, develop callouses, and raise the price. "The only reason there are leather handles on racquets," he told writer George Plimpton at the Forest Hills nationals in 1975, "is that years back L. B. Isely, the president of Wilson's Sporting Goods, got up at a meeting and said, 'Hey, look here, why don't we dress up a tennis racquet like a golf club and put leather handles on it and charge a dollar more.' Everybody agreed it was a fine idea. So the result is that you see players scratching up the leather to get a better grip, coming down with blisters and callouses. The consistency of leather changes; leather absorbs 87 percent of the moisture, compared to seven percent for wood. Bill Tilden knew it was crazy. He and I were the only ones to stick to wood. He used to say, 'For God's sake, Don, you and I are the only ones left. Don't tell anyone.' "

Budge was a rare bird accorded the blessing of the crusty old USLTA when he deserted amateur ranks at the peak of his game. Ordinarily, in the eras leading up to the 1970s officials of the ruling body brooked professionals as they would brook the Bubonic plague. But in Budge's case, though his departure clearly clarioned a loss of the Davis Cup after a mere two years, the president of the USLTA, Holcombe Ward, even called a press conference in New York to announce Budge's decision and to confer the association's blessing. By contrast, Tilden, Vines, and Vincent Richards had been ostracized by the panjandrums when they turned pro.

But Budge was something else. After his big sweep of 1937 he had staunchly resisted the pros, turning down a $50,000 minimum offer to tour with Perry on the old-fashioned (and apparently heartfelt) grounds that he still owed his loyalty to the USLTA. That summer he had led the assault against Germany in the inter-zone challenge round, beating von Cramm in the key match, and then had gone into the challenge round against the defending champion British team partnered by Frankie Parker in singles and Gene Mako in doubles.

Here, Parker split with Bunny Austin and Charlie Hare, but Budge whipped both soundly, then teamed with Mako for the 4–1 victory that meant the return of the trophy. Earlier that month he had created a Wimbledon shambles, winning the singles over von Cramm, teaming with Mako to take the men's doubles, and combining with Alice Marble to win the mixed. Then at

58

Forest Hills, he whistled into the final of the U.S. nationals without loss of a set and scored his third straight triumph of that gilded season over von Cramm. Since he was clearly the best of the amateurs, there was high public interest in whether he had caught up to Perry and there was little doubt their matching would have produced record gates. But he declined, and the USLTA was properly grateful.

As it turned out, Budge did himself a favor, too. He was even more successful in 1938 than he'd been a year earlier because he scored his unprecedented Grand Slam, an achievement matched in succeeding years only by Rod Laver in 1962 and 1969. In truth, though, when the Australians got their first look at Budge on his arrival Down Under late in 1937 they were far from impressed. He engaged in several minor tournaments leading up to the Australian, the first Grand Slam leg, and lost eight of his first ten matches. What the Aussie public didn't know was that Budge had been forewarned by fellow Americans Wilmer Allison, John Van Ryn, and Ellsworth Vines to sharpen his game in the early events, building slowly to the big one. Accordingly, he was in top form, doing road work and exercising regularly, and not even the excessive heat of Australia in January, ranging from 105 to 115 degrees, could dissuade him in the biggest championship. He whipped John Bromwich in the final by 6–3, 6–1, 6–2.

On the slow red clay of the Roland Garros Stadium in Paris in June, Budge was impressive. "I wanted to prove that my game was equally the same on all surfaces," he said later of the French Championships. "Conditions are different in tournaments all over the world (and) I suffered throughout from a stomach disorder." Nonetheless, he lost only two sets in getting halfway through his Slam, and was so dominant that in encountering what he described as "one of the greatest thrills of my life," he wasn't talking about tennis, at all, but in meeting the cello virtuoso, Pablo Casals. "We always had tea together after my singles," he wrote later, "and after the final he said, 'Don, I got so much enjoyment from watching you play that I would like to invite you back to my house tonight to play for you.' I accepted with great enthusiasm, and after dinner ten of us climbed up to Pablo's studio overlooking Paris and sat on the floor as he played to the rapture of all of us for some two hours."

Wimbledon was nothing less than a rout. Budge didn't lose a set working through to the final, and then simply toyed with Bunny Austin in the final by 6–1, 6–0, 6–3. That left only Forest Hills to complete the Slam, and again Budge was invincible. He met his doubles partner, Gene Mako, in the final and won in four sets, completing an unbeaten season that stretched back to Australia in January. It was to this feat that Walter Pate referred in rating Budge's success superior to that of Bobby Jones. Budge ended his season with two defeats on the West Coast, losing anticlimactic matches to Aussies Adrian Quist and Harry Hopman in the Pacific Southwest and the Pacific Coast tournaments. Late in the fall, Budge was voted by American sportswriters as the country's top athlete, amateur or pro. So with the Davis Cup defended and the boards swept clean, there were obviously no more amateur peaks for him to ascend. The USLTA blessed him.

As a youth, curiously, Budge had no interest in tennis,

even scorned it as a game for twits. He was a good ball-player, a tough left-hand hitter, a fact that in later years helped account for the most remarkable backhand stroke in tennis. The swing was the same; he guided his back-swing with his left hand and kept that hand on the rac-quet as he came through to meet the ball, letting go at the moment of impact. "His backhand had that extra flair, that great freedom of motion, which made it the envy of every player who ever lived," Julius Heldman once wrote. "His forte was sustained power, not touch tennis. He could hit a placement from any spot in the court to any other spot in the court."

But when Budge was growing up in Oakland these en-comiums were a long way off. He played basketball and football and *some* tennis, but only because his brother Lloyd was a tennis nut. Lloyd, four years older, could persuade Don to hit a few exchanges with him, but the lanky redhead soon grew bored and headed for the ball field. The Budges were a family of modest means. Don's father, John, had moved to California for his health, emi-grating from Scotland where he'd played world-class soc-cer for the renowned Glasgow Rangers. He was injured once, developed pneumonia and then bronchitis, and went to America's West Coast where he met and married Irish-born Pearl Kincaid and where they raised their two sons and a daughter Jean.

Don was fifteen when he got turned around on tennis. Disdaining the game, he was chided during the family dinner one June night in 1930 by brother Lloyd for de-clining to join him in the California state boys' champion-ships a week hence. Annoyed or challenged or dismayed or whatever, he impulsively decided to go into the tournament, practiced for a week and, performing in corduroy pants, rushed through to the finals. His father hurriedly ran a pair of old white ducks through a laundry he managed in Oakland in time for the big match, and the boy responded in his resplendent trappings by winning, at 6–4, 6–0, the first tournament he'd ever entered. The experience was exhilarating; three years later, at eighteen, he won both the senior and junior California championships in the same season. The grateful Northern California Association sent him to Culver, Indiana, for the national junior championships and were rewarded for their pains and money when he beat the best of Southern California's juniors in the final, a young lad named Gene Mako.

He went East to play the grass-court circuit when he was nineteen, touring the fussy and fashionable resorts of Rye and Seabright, Newport and Longwood, and making his first appearance at Forest Hills. He was impressive in none of these; yet, as it turned out, his game made an impact upon the one man in the best position to advance his career rapidly—Walter Pate. "His forehand needs work," Pate allowed, "but he's the fellow we need to bring back the Davis Cup."

A few months later Pate was made team captain and one of the conditions on which he took the assignment was that Budge, ranked no higher than ninth that year, be assigned to the squad ahead of older players who had been losing to France and England—Sidney Wood and Frank Shields, among others. "We aren't going to win it overnight," Pate noted, "and that young man will be ready in a couple of years."

Wood accepted the situation most graciously. He

helped straighten out the serious problems of Budge's forehand, urging him to stop experimenting with grips and to settle on one. Tom Stow, coach at the University of California, worked through the winter with Budge, and even the Briton, Fred Perry, came along with tips on the young man's footwork. In time, he mastered the balky forehand, developing what Julius Heldman was to describe as a technically flawless "relentless bludgeon."

But his skills were still only burgeoning in 1935, though at twenty he was unmistakably on his way. When Pate joined him with top-ranked veteran Wilmer Allison in Davis Cup singles against Australia, he rushed into a two-set lead over the world's No. 2 player behind Perry, the stylish Jack Crawford. In his inexperience he let up on an early aggressiveness and when his game came down a notch he was caught by the Aussie. In a draining fifth set in 105-degree heat in Philadelphia, Crawford got ahead 5–3 but Budge wiggled from this precarious situation, and they went to 11–11 before Budge managed to end the four-hour and ten-minute match. It was a last-gasp effort. "Leg cramps had finished me," he said. "But as I hobbled from the court I heard a murmur from the crowd. I looked around. Crawford had passed out cold."

The win qualified the Americans for overseas play against Germany and, winning again, they met the British for the Cup. It was a disaster. Perry and Bunny Austin won four singles matches from Budge and Allison, and the Brits beat the doubles combination of Budge and Mako without trouble. Still, as Pate had said, success was going to take longer than overnight.

By this time Mako, an affable and uninhibited fellow of warm and outgoing nature, had helped Budge overcome his shyness in meeting people, especially girls. The pair became close friends, drove their dates to dances where Benny Goodman and Tommy Dorsey played things like "Begin the Beguine" and "I'll Never Cry Again." Sometimes the young tennis stars joined the musicians and played the drums.

On the courts, Budge grew taller. Soon there was no one around, apart from Perry, who could handle him. Still, Perry was enough. He led Britain to another Davis Cup in 1936 and blocked Budge's path at Wimbledon in four sets and at Forest Hills in five. There, Budge got two sets ahead and even by 5–3 in the fifth but couldn't hold on. At the end of that season, though, when Perry turned pro, it was obvious Budge's time had arrived, and in the summer of 1937 he won Wimbledon without fuss. Accordingly, he seemed likely to lead the way to the long-awaited return of the Davis Cup when, with the jangle of a telephone bell, there developed one of the most dramatic moments in international tennis history.

Center court at Wimbledon glowed in sunshine and the swirl of a colorful overflow crowd. Queen Mary and her entourage festooned the royal box. Here was the final day of singles between the U.S. and Germany, the winner almost certain to wrest the Davis Cup. England was the defending champion, awaiting the survivor, but with Perry gone England was conceded small chance.

So now it was up to Budge and von Cramm, matched in a decisive instant. The sides were deadlocked at two wins each and as the players were about to emerge side by side from the locker room a telephone rang.

"Mr. von Cramm," an attendant called. "Long distance for you, sir."

He hesitated.

"It might be an emergency," he said, deciding to take the call.

"Yes, hello, this is Gottfried Cramm."

Moments later he switched to German. *"Ja, mein Fuhrer,"* he said tautly.

He said little else but *"Ja, mein Fuhrer,"* for the rest of the conversation. Then, face grim, he hung up.

"Excuse me, gentlemen," he said to Budge and others there, "it was Hitler. I don't know why he called me."

Hitler's call placed enormous pressure on the baron, widely known to be anti-Nazi in a time of feverish military nationalism within Germany. Physically, he was the embodiment of Hitler's unconscionable theory of Nordic-type racial superiority—tall, blond, blue-eyed, athletic. And, of course, the Fuhrer's athletes had not been reflecting his racial theories: Jesse Owens, the black American, was the dominant figure in 1936 at what Hitler had hoped would be his world showcase, the Berlin Olympics. More, Joe Louis had avenged a 12th-round knockout by the German Max Schmeling, pulverizing Schmeling in the first round of the rematch. Here now, the Fuhrer felt, was von Cramm's opportunity to restore a vestige of national honor, a role von Cramm loathed (indeed, a year later he was arrested by the Gestapo for anti-party activity).

This, then, was the turbulent setting for the match some have called the most dramatic and in some ways the finest Davis Cup encounter ever played, one that had other curious overtones apart from the Hitler involvement. For instance, the coach of the German team was Bill Tilden, a questionable role for the controversial

American pro, not so much because he had agreed to help a foreign team—nothing uncommon there—but that he had perhaps tactlessly retained the post after the Germans eliminated Czechoslovakia to qualify to meet Tilden's own countrymen, and particularly in the delicate political climate of the period. Tilden was a highly visible figure as the match began, seated along the sideline immediately in front of a tiny American delegation, the comedian Jack Benny, the columnist Ed Sullivan, and the transplanted Hungarian actor Paul Lukas.

To favored Budge's dismay, von Cramm won the first two sets. Budge had been well back in matches before this one, assuredly, but what annoyed him this time was that he felt he'd rarely played better than now. His shots were whistling—but they were coming back. His service was a cannonball—but it was coming back. His backhand was lifting chalk from the tapes—but it was coming back. Not always, of course; but too often. Leading 5–4 and serving for the set, he hit four consecutive first-serve bullets. Von Cramm returned every one for a placement. "The only thing I hit in that game was beautiful first serves," he said later. "I never touched a single return." Four games later, von Cramm broke him again to win that first set at 8–6. And then the German won the second, 7–5, both players still reeling off flat-out shots. Budge prevented a rout by pulling out the third set at 6–4.

Von Cramm was lifeless in the fourth after Budge broke him twice in the first three games, perhaps deciding to conserve energy for the fifth set. He was a notoriously strong finisher; in the French Championships a year earlier after prevailing in several five-set matches he had hit a peak performance in the final, pulverizing Fred Perry 6–0 in the fifth set.

Now it appeared he was bent on beating Budge in a similar manner. Serving first, he got a 2–1 lead as each held service, then broke Budge, held again, and thus owned a 4–1 advantage. As Budge went to the baseline to serve the sixth game, his eye caught the form of Bill Tilden at the sideline. Tilden was signaling to von Cramm's singles partner, Henner Henkel, sitting a few rows back of the Americans Benny, Sullivan, and Lukas. Budge was startled by what he saw, as he wrote in *A Tennis Memoir* in 1969: "Tilden could not contain himself (with von Cramm leading 4–1). He stood up in his seat and turned fully around, looking past Benny and Sullivan and Lukas to where Henkel was sitting. Then, without a word, only a large smug grin on his face, he held up his hand, forming a circle with his thumb and forefinger—the traditional 'It's in the bag' sign. Sullivan and the others saw it right away and were furious. Immediately, Sullivan leaped to his feet and began to try to tear his coat off, at the same time hissing imprecations at Tilden. Lukas and Benny jumped up themselves and managed to pull Sullivan down and hold him. Tilden just smiled back and then sat down again."

In retrospect, it does not appear that the byplay had an effect on Budge, even psychologically. He was three games down, there was sideline emotional involvement, but realistically he recognized he trailed by only one service break and felt strong. He knew, of course, that he was through if von Cramm won each of his next two turns at service but he was philosophical enough to realize that he still had two chances to break the German's serve once and be even—provided, of course, he held his own serve.

This he did, at love, in the sixth game. With von Cramm serving, he decided to attack the German's second service, given the chance, by moving in and taking it on the rise. As luck would have it—or the pressure on von Cramm—the baron kept missing with that first serve by the narrowest of margins. Each time, Budge crowded the second serve, took it on the rise, drove it deep, and followed to the net for a winning volley. Von Cramm got his first serve in only once, and that was the only point he won as Budge crept to 3–4, then held service to tie at four each. They then split the next four games to go to 6–6 and then Budge broke von Cramm to lead for the first time in the match.

There followed the longest game of the long, long match. Fifteen-love, fifteen-all, thirty-fifteen, thirty-all, forty-thirty (a match point for Budge), then deuce. It went on for minutes that way, point after point, deuce after deuce. Budge had four runs at match point, von Cramm two at tying the set 7–7. Then Budge got a fifth opportunity. He served strongly but von Cramm hammered a deep return and a baseline exchange ensued. Budge, moved to the left side of his court, put a backhand down the line, not deep, and von Cramm pounced. He laced a crosscourt forehand far to Budge's right, then running to his left, to follow his shot to the net, cutting off Budge's angle of return.

Budge had recognized as soon as his backhand had fallen short that von Cramm was in perfect position to

crosscourt him. He was already running flat out, anticipating the return, trying to cover the far sideline.

"I did the only thing I could," he wrote in *A Tennis
Memoir*. "I kept going at full speed and just took a swipe
at the ball. There was no way I could keep from falling
. . . I could tell, though, as soon as I hit the ball that I
had smacked it solidly, but only as I crashed into the
grass did I turn to look."

He had hit the ball into the only opening von Cramm
had been unable to cover—directly down the German's
left sideline. Von Cramm's frantic lunge for a volley
missed by inches. The ball hugged the inside of the tape.
Von Cramm didn't turn to watch its flight; he knew it was
good. He waited for Budge to climb to his feet and reach
the net. He threw his arms around Budge's shoulders. He
said it was the finest match he had ever played. A year
later he was in a Nazi prison and Budge was completing
the first Grand Slam in tennis history.

Bobby Riggs

BOBBY RIGGS

[1918–   ]

*D*ECORUM AND CONVENTION were never words that appealed very much to Bobby Riggs, who played tennis surpassingly well in an era when decorum and convention were as much a part of the game as white tennis balls and real grass courts.

Riggs owes his modern renown to a couple of hammy matches with Margaret Court and Billie Jean King in 1973, but thirty-odd years earlier he was as spectacularly nonconformist—and good, too.

Indeed, maybe he was great. "He did everything right," the analyst of style, Julius Heldman, remembers. "He was undoubtedly the cagiest player of all time. More than any other player, he exemplified the champion's will to win."

Riggs won the U.S. national singles title twice at Forest Hills and swept the boards at Wimbledon in 1939 when he won the singles as well as men's and mixed doubles. In 1946 and 1947 he was the best professional player alive.

When Riggs was growing up in his native Southern California he ran afoul of that area's dictatorial tennis head Perry Jones who, as Riggs saw things, was more concerned about a youngster's family background than his tennis ability. He liked young players to be tall, immaculate in white tennis clothes, respectfully polite, and to come from Pasadena or Beverly Hills or one of the other fashionable districts of Los Angeles. Riggs fit none of these descriptions. He stopped growing at a half-inch under five-eight, often turned up to play tennis in street clothes and sneakers and, though he wasn't disrespectful, he was outspoken about what he considered Perry Jones's discrimination. On top of that, he bet on himself to win matches even in his mid-teens. Indeed, if he didn't have a bet going when he played he tended to lose interest. In his first visit to Wimbledon in 1939 when he was twenty-one and had succeeded Don Budge as America's top player, he set out to find a bookmaker before the tournament began. He located one in Fleet Street.

"What are the odds on this fellow Riggs to win the men's singles?" he inquired of a gnarled little Londoner with a tweed cap in back of the counter in one of the legal betting shops.

"Let me see. 'Ere now, 'e's three to one."

"Three to one!" cried Riggs. "But it's his first try at Wimbledon. The odds ought to be twice that."

"No, 'e's number one in the U.S.," said the imperturbable bookie. "Three to one's quite sufficient."

So Riggs bet a hundred pounds on himself at a time when the British pound was worth about five U.S. dollars.

Still unsatisfied with his action, Riggs asked the bookie what odds he'd lay against Bobby winning the men's doubles if he won the single and let his money ride.

"Six to one."

"Six to one! But Riggs and Elwood Cooke were beaten in the French Championships by two old guys, Borotra and Brugnon."

The bookie suppressed a yawn. "Six to one," he repeated.

"Okay, okay. But what if Riggs gets lucky, wins the singles and doubles, and I parlay the bundle onto him and Alice Marble on the mixed?"

"For a bet like that, it's twelve to one."

"Not enough."

"Sorry."

"Oh, all right."

So Riggs left the shop with his hundred-pound bet, odds of three to one on the singles parlayed at six to one on the men's doubles and twelve to one if his money were still alive for the mixed.

Bobby swept through the early rounds of Wimbledon without difficulty and reached the final opposite his doubles partner Cooke. "I've always believed the incentive of the parlay made the difference," he wrote in his autobiography, *Court Hustler,* reflecting on the match. "I was down two sets to one when I thought about my investment. That was sufficient to spur me into taking the last two sets."

He and Cooke then combined to beat England's Charlie Hare and Frank Wilde in the doubles final. Meanwhile, Alice Marble was building up a pressure-cooker of her own. She won the singles, partnered Sarah Fabyan to win the doubles, and now found herself, like Riggs, just one step removed from the rare triple triumph. They pulled it off, too, in straight sets. Alice was delighted to embrace her three pieces of silverware, but Riggs could scarcely wait for Monday morning to rush into Fleet Street and claim his far richer rewards—21,600 English pounds which converted into about $108,000 in American funds. "It was the biggest bet I ever won on myself in tennis," Riggs wrote, not surprisingly. In the inflationary market of the mid-1970s the amount translated into about half a million dollars.

Still, Bobby did a lot of sweating before he could lay hands on the money. As an amateur, he was reluctant to open a bank account of such staggering proportions so he placed the money in a vault in a London bank, planning to claim it the following year when he turned professional. But in September 1939, of course, World War II began, and wartime restrictions prevented him from removing his pounds from the country. No one, not even Sir Winston Churchill, was more relieved when Germany capitulated in 1945.

Bobby was the youngest of five brothers whose father was a minister in a strict fundamentalist church that frowned on almost all forms of human enjoyment, even the playing of organ music. As often happens, the boys rebelled against the strict yoke of imposed denial, though sports proved a healthy outlet for their energies and they avoided trouble. Bobby began gambling to provide himself with tennis equipment, mostly balls, playing for new ones when he didn't have a dime in his pockets. He learned to study his opponents closely so that he never played a kid until he figured he could beat him. He was wiry, quick on his feet and a fast learner, and his brothers helped him become a game competitor.

One day when he was twelve and playing tennis with an older brother, a woman named Dr. Esther Bartosh, the third-ranking woman in Los Angeles and an instructor at the University of Southern California, stopped to watch. Something about the way Bobby played appealed to her athletic eye, and she offered to teach him to hit the ball properly.

He had been playing with a borrowed racquet that day but now, with his own private instructor, he recognized the need to acquire one of his own. He did it the way he knew best: he played marbles with a kid whose sister had a racquet she never used. When he cleaned the kid out of marbles, the kid began to ponder ways of getting his marbles back. What should he happen to remember but his sister's tennis racquet? And who should be willing to trade back the marbles for it? In no time at all, Bobby Riggs had his first racquet.

Dr. Bartosh worked on his game for two years during which he never lost a match in the thirteen-and-under bracket. She developed in him the fundamentals for every stroke, the correct footwork, the basic strategy. Years later, assessing his form, Julius Heldman wrote: "Bobby Riggs's forehand was absolutely correct in every particular. . . . (He) was just as letter-perfect on the backhand . . . His was the most underrated serve in the game. . . . As a pro he made the volley his forte . . . was lethal on short to medium lobs (with his overhead smash) and careful on the deep ones. . . . He was a clutch artist, a money player and a competitor who was never out of the match until the last point was over."

Dr. Bartosh gave him the philosophy that served him throughout his career, and one that is effective for any tennis player of modest physical power: "Tennis matches are won on mistakes. Let the other fellow hit the ball too

75

hard. Let the other fellow hit the ball into the net. Let the other fellow make the mistakes. It's not how hard you hit the ball but *where* you hit it."

She also taught him to be a good loser as well as a good winner. Accordingly, he accepted bad calls as part of the game—"like sun in your eyes or a windy day"—and all through his career he never questioned a call by a linesman or argued a decision with an umpire.

Riggs piled success upon success all through his teens. He won the California State High School championship three years in a row, a record still unmatched in the mid-1970s, and at seventeen he expanded his horizons to win the National Junior championship in 1935. He played the sensational serve-and-volley star Joe Hunt in scores of finals and in one stretch won seventeen of them in a row, including the national junior crown. There, a wealthy tennis buff announced he'd pay the expenses of the winner to Wimbledon, so Riggs was ecstatic when he beat Hunt in the final. But the sponsor backed off.

"I'm sorry, Bobby," he said unhappily. "The Southern California association has wired me to call off the Wimbledon trip. I don't like to argue with those boys." The decision was, to Riggs, another illustration of the discrimination of Perry Jones, further exemplified a year later when Jones refused to provide expense money and official sponsorship for Riggs on the eastern grass-court circuit.

But Riggs went anyway. He and a junior from Oregon, Wayne Sabin, were sponsored by a fun-loving fellow named Jack Del Valle, who drove them east in his Cadillac and handled the side-bets for Bobby, strolling around the courts and marking the "action" in a small black notebook.

Riggs won the singles and he and Sabin the doubles in a tournament in Kansas City, then moved on to the National Clay Courts championships in Chicago. They repeated their Kansas City sweep there, and Del Valle was the busiest book man in Chicago.

Sponsors of grass-court tournaments on the eastern seaboard now fell over themselves to attract the rising young West Coaster to their events, in spite of letters from Perry Jones in California saying that he was to be given no special considerations. Even tiny tournaments such as one in Neenah, Wisconsin, paid him $500 cash, plus full accommodations, hotel and meals, and transportation, to attract his entry. To validate the hypocrisy, tournament chairmen would bet him large amounts that he couldn't jump over the tennis net. He went on the payroll of the Wall Street broker Edmund C. Lynch at $200 a week, played tennis with him and his friends at their estates in Miami, Nassau, and Long Island, and travelled on Lynch's yacht. When Lynch died Riggs was given another $200-a-week "job" by L. B. Isely, president of the Wilson Sporting Goods company, who moved him to Chicago and had him placed on the advertising account of Red Heart Dog Food at the agency that handled Wilson's advertising. Amateurism was a giant sham and Riggs deplored it, laughing all the way to the bank.

Still, the discrimination persisted. By 1937 Riggs was clearly the No. 2 player in the country behind Don Budge but the USLTA people refused to name him to the Davis Cup team. Indeed, that year he was allowed to practice with Budge and the rest before they left for England but not permitted to accompany the team overseas though he could beat everybody who went, apart from Budge.

By 1938, though, with Budge on the brink of turning professional, it was impossible to keep Riggs on the sidelines. He delivered a key victory in the 3–2 U.S. margin over Australia, beating Adrian Quist in four sets. The next year, with Budge gone, he partnered Frank Parker in the singles assignments against the Aussies and beat Jack Bromwich on opening day. But Quist handled him in five sets to square the series, and Bromwich's victory over Parker sent the trophy Down Under for the duration of World War II.

In spite of the defeat by Quist, 1939 was Riggs's biggest year as an amateur. In Paris for the French Championships he sampled the good life on the Left Bank, of the Folies Bergère and of the Lido on the Champs d'Elysees, and still managed to reach the final round on the Roland Garros clay courts. There, countryman Don McNeill clobbered him. There too, he and Elwood Cooke lost the men's doubles final to the fading French team of Jean Borotra and Jacques Brugnon. Obviously, he was undaunted by these setbacks, for this was the summer that he sped to the bookmakers in Fleet Street to multiply his hundred-pound bet a thousandfold. Winning everything in sight at Wimbledon, he moved on to Forest Hills in September and won his first U.S. national singles crown, as well.

With Budge, Ellsworth Vines, and Britain's Fred Perry dominating the pro tours Riggs delayed his own leap from the amateurs in 1940, hoping to build up his value by repeating at Forest Hills (he couldn't improve on his reputation or his bankroll at Wimbledon again; the war had closed down the famous old tennis hutch). But it was a blank year; he and Frank Parker blew the Davis Cup to the Aussies and, worse, he lost the Forest Hills final to McNeill. That meant postponing his professional aspirations until he could recapture the U.S. crown, and he did that by beating a young screwball named Frankie Kovacs, perhaps an even more successful psyche artist than Riggs himself. Bobby went onto the court one time wearing shorts, an unusual departure from the traditional cream colored flannels of the era, and Kovacs kept pointing to them and laughing uproariously. Then he sped to the locker room between sets for a pair of scissors, and returned to courtside and cut off his flannels above his knobby knees. Riggs couldn't concentrate, couldn't keep a straight face, and couldn't win.

But Riggs got even at Forest Hills. He dropped the first set at 7–5, then came back to win the next two easily. He wanted to prevent Kovacs from having a consultation with his coach during the intermission after the third set because he had Frankie on the run and didn't want him to change tactics.

So he sidled alongside Kovacs, who had slumped to a chair at the sideline after the third set, and casually toweling himself remarked idly: "You look tired, Frankie. I guess you want to go in and lie down awhile."

Kovacs was instantly affronted.

"Tired? Who's tired? Hey, let's get out there and finish this."

Thus, they skipped the intermission and Riggs, clucking inwardly, finished off Frankie by 6–3. A week later he signed a $25,000 contract to join the professional tour against Fred Perry.

But nothing went right. Nineteen days before the tour was to start in New York, the Japanese bombed Pearl Harbor, and people stayed away from touring tennis in droves, minds turned suddenly elsewhere. Making dismal matters worse, Perry injured his right elbow in a fall soon after the series began and had to retire. His replacements lacked appeal, though they were changed repeatedly, and the tour died of the financial shorts when twenty stops still remained on the schedule.

Five years later, after VJ-Day, Riggs finally asserted his supremacy over the world's pros by beating Budge in international tours in 1946 and 1947. But coming up on the outside like a challenging thoroughbred was the newest bright star of tennis, the Californian with the Big Game—Jack Kramer. They were matched in a long and successful world tour that opened on the snowswept night of December 26, 1947, in Madison Square Garden. There, in spite of a record snowfall, a full house stared in disbelief as unpredictable Riggs fooled everyone by racing to the net behind every serve, abandoning his celebrated retriever tactics and, alternately, throwing lobs up into the lights to confound the rookie pro in four sets. He also picked off $5000 in bets, delaying the start of the match while he booked last-minute action at courtside.

Riggs did all right through thirty matches on the tour as the strong young Kramer gradually got his big game into high gear. Bobby trailed by sixteen matches to fourteen at that point, but by then his arm began to wear down under the constant and unaccustomed pounding of a volleying game, and Kramer tore him to pieces thereafter.

He promoted the tour for a couple of years, then undertook a second marriage, this one to Priscilla Wheelan whose wealthy family owned the American Photograph Corporation and he settled down with her in Florida where he discovered golf. Riggs and golf—a game of almost limitless gambling opportunities—were made for each other. As Bobby noted one time, "The second worst thing in the world is betting on a golf game and losing; the worst is not betting at all." Golf's handicapping system, in which poor golfers are not necessarily unable to beat good golfers if the handicaps are properly weighted, provided Riggs with sixteen years of endless betting possibilities, and he explored them all.

But tennis was the game he liked most, and he returned to it when he turned forty-five in 1963 and was living in New York. In friendly matches his pals imposed ridiculous handicaps upon him—carrying an open umbrella, leading a dog on a leash, carrying a suitcase in his left hand. Through all these innovations his betting never flagged.

By the time he was fifty-one a seniors' circuit had been organized featuring his peers, Gardner Mulloy, Vic Seixas, Tom Brown, Jaroslav Drobny, and Frank Sedgman, among others. By then, too, a women's circuit was burgeoning, and it galled Riggs that the women were attracting more prize money than the seniors. He was convinced a good old boy could beat a good young girl, any place, any time, any kind of weather. He offered to bet Billie Jean King, the reigning woman, that he could beat her for $5000, winner take all, but she brushed him off.

He threw the same bait to Margaret Court, the tall, hard-hitting Australian, and she bit.

They played on Mother's Day at San Diego Estates in California in May 1973, and as Bobby modestly phrased it after he'd psyched her out of her tennis socklets and beaten her in straight sets, "I had become the hero of all middle-aged men smarting under the taunts of the Women's Libbers, the leader of Bobby's Battalions, and the undisputed number-one male chauvinist in the world."

Now Billie Jean was forced from the woodwork to meet this fifty-five-year-old opportunist and defend the enormous advances made by the women pros. They were matched in the Houston Astrodome in September for $100,000, winner take all, in a goofy confrontation that captured the human lunacy like hula-hoops and yo-yos and guys swallowing goldfish. Riggs played his role to the hilt. The weeks and days leading up to the match were marvellous ones for him. All of a sudden, at age fifty-five with one foot in the grave (a phrase he pounded relentlessly) he had an audience. There was small evidence, of course, that in all of those fifty-five years he'd ever stopped talking, but the difference now was that people stayed and listened to him instead of emptying rooms whenever he opened his mouth. Was Bobby grateful to the women's liberation movement, which made it all possible? No way.

"U.S. women are the most privileged in history and they want more," he droned on one day at the Westside Racquet Club in Beverly Hills after a practice session. "Young guys getting married can't do anything. They're becoming enslaved. I'm playing Billie Jean for all the

82

guys who are gonna get married, whose wives won't let them play poker on Friday night or go fishin' on the weekend. I've gotta do it, an old guy fifty-five years old with one foot in the grave. There wouldn't be any world problems if women had stayed in the kitchen and the bedroom.

"Billie Jean's friend, Rosemary Casals, says I can't see, I can't hear, I walk like a duck and besides that I'm an idiot. But I'm gonna beat their best player, that Billie Jean King; it'll be like taking candy from a baby. I'll toy with that girl. And if I can do that, an old guy of fifty-five with one foot in the grave, where does that leave them?"

He brayed on and on—and on—that day at the West-side Racquet Club. A mile and a half north was 20th Century-Fox on Pico Boulevard and a mile and a half south were Metro Goldwyn Mayer and David O. Selznick Studios on Washington Boulevard. In the old days, when Bobby was a boy growing up nearby, movie people flocked from these big studios to play tennis at this club, but by 1973 the big studios weren't very big and the movie business had all changed. By 1973 the Westside Racquet Club had become a private club with a $2500 initiation fee and dues of $75 a month. Its eight smooth ersatz courts were painted green with white lines, and the clubhouse was California Spanish, flat-roofed and sprawling, with pools and patios and saunas and bars.

Bobby Riggs, the super hustler, often went there as his match with Billie Jean approached, ostensibly to practice but really to hustle the match and to revel in the sudden spotlight so long gone. With him most days was a young Las Vegas pro named Lornie Kuhle who described himself as Bobby's "trainer and sort of manager; he's like a

83

father to me," and in his party were Jerry Perenchio, the promoter of the Houston caper; a little round guy named Jackie Barnett, the executive producer for ABC television's involvement in it; Bobby's seventeen-year-old son Billy, who stared bemused at the hoopla; an actress friend of Bobby's named Sandra Giles, a braless girl who described herself as emancipated but who, in spite of these two factors, had bet $200 on Bobby to beat Billie Jean; and a squadron of teen-age girls hired by a Hollywood ad agency to follow Bobby around, fawn on him, and never be seen in public without cotton T-shirts that proclaimed in tall lettering I LOVE BOBBY.

Assembled to meet this coterie was a horde of wretches from the media, weighted down with TV shoulder cameras, whirring boxes of film, coils of trailing cables, Nikons and strobes, microphones, tape recorders, and writing pads and ballpoints.

"Okay, fellahs, what else do you want?" Riggs cried to this mob. "Is that it? Is there anything else? Anybody want to get me signing my book? My new book, brought out by Lippincott? The story of my life? It came out the first of the month, people can get it at bookstores anywhere. Hey, tell everybody to run out and get my new book. Can we get a shot of me holding it?"

Somebody asked him if he was ready for Billie Jean.

"Not yet, not yet, but I will be. I'm taking my vitamin pills, 415 of 'em a day, an old guy fifty-five years of age with one foot in the grave, but I'll be ready for her. She has the strength of ten men. She won all three finals in one day at Wimbledon. She has such a fantastic ego you can't believe it. She's playin' for a cause, for all those women who want to keep guys from playin' poker on Friday night and fishin' on weekends, all the young guys just gettin' married."

He talked and talked, moving along, surrounded by media people, radio guys taping radio interviews, TV guys standing with an arm slung across his shoulders while cameramen taped TV interviews, newspaper guys tugging at his sleeve, grinning all the time, answering everybody, picking up thoughts in mid-sentence and belting out answers . . . "All the guys who are gonna get married . . . fifty-five-year-old guy with one foot in the grave . . . be no problems if women'd stay in the kitchen and the bedroom . . . Rosemary Casals says I can't see, I can't hear . . . vitamin pills . . . battle of the sexes . . . why shouldn't they let me into women's tournaments; everybody knows there's no sex after fifty-five . . . she's gonna have a lot of pressure on her . . . girls say they should get as much money as men." On and on, never running down, glorying in it, reacting to questions as though he'd been programmed, as though somebody had turned on a tape-recorder button at play and couldn't find the off button.

His son Billy was asked what the old gentleman with one foot in the grave was like before he turned to playing women tennis players for a living.

The young man, detached from the hubbub, carrying a book called *The Art of Meditation* by Joel S. Goldsmith under his arm, grinned slowly. "Ah, he was just like he is now, a big ego," he said amiably. "Except nobody listened then."

The promoter Perenchio, who'd put up $100,000 for

the winner, noted that the winner-take-all aspect of the match didn't mean the loser would go away in sackcloth and ashes.

"Ancillary rights," he expanded. "Ancillary rights will provide a hundred thousand each for them. The other hundred thousand's on top of that. We sold out TV sponsorship a week ago, fifteen minutes at $80,000 a minute. Cadillac alone bought five minutes. The Astrodome is scaled to a $700,000 gate, 55,000 people with a hundred-dollar top. Everybody'll do just fine."

The actress Sandra Giles said that even apart from her two-hundred dollar bet she wanted Bobby to win and that a lot of other women did, too.

"I'm a happy woman," she said. "There are equal opportunities for women if they'll pursue them. I like men to be strong. They shouldn't be dominated, shouldn't let themselves be. I felt this way before women's lib came along. I threw away the bra; it's attractive on me—or off me, I guess I mean."

Riggs was loose again. "What have I got against women's lib? Nothing. I'm just pro men's lib. I've been married twice and divorced twice. I've escaped twice. And what's happening now is just great, being the instant celebrity, making endorsements, all this stuff. I'm an old guy fifty-five years old with one foot in the grave and if I beat Billie Jean it'll be for all the guys who are gonna get married . . ."

Thirty-five thousand people showed up in the Astrodome. Billie Jean King beat Bobby Riggs in straight sets. Millions of people watched on television. It was one hell of a long way from center court at Wimbledon.

JACK KRAMER

[1921–   ]

$\mathcal{B}$IG JAKE they called him—Jack Kramer, a hard man
to miss on or off the tennis court, the guy who revolutionized the game when he played it and who gave it a
whole new dimension when he turned to the promotion
of it.

Big Jake. He oozed energy. You could feel it in a room
or on a court. Barely contained emotion itching to get
loose. A hard twinkle in the eye. An edginess. "Hey, let's
get this show on the road." If Big Jake didn't invent that
line, he should have. Near him, you could feel the vibra-
tions, a man who had to get up and get going.

And cold. Ice cold. Lots of fun and games and a nice
sense of humor but then, with the match on the line or
the money on the table, nerveless. Controlled aggres-
sion.

He won everything. At seventeen he was a Davis Cupper. World War II interrupted his climb for two years.
Barely out of uniform, impatient to get back to the game,
he wrecked an uncalloused hand gripping new tennis
racquets at Wimbledon and lost in the first post-war tournament there to the wily Czech Jaroslav Drobny. But
after that he was untouchable. He won the national singles at Forest Hills twice, returned to Wimbledon to win

Jack Kramer

there, won the U.S. doubles four times with Ted Schroeder, the Wimbledon doubles with Tom Brown and then
Bob Falkenburg, defended the Davis Cup, unbeaten, and
with no one left to challenge him seriously he turned pro
and instantly dominated the tours of that era. He scuttled
Bobby Riggs, embarrassed a too young Pancho Gonzales,
then turned promoter himself and continued to prosper
on the court, walloping Frank Sedgman and whipping
Pancho Segura. Then he retired as a player and turned
his enormous energy toward broadening the professional
base with open tournaments and to removing the hypocrisy of shamateurism.

He turned the game around in the latter part of the
1940s. "The Kramer theory of modern tennis completely
changed the complexion of the game," wrote the percep-
tive and analytical Julius Heldman in *Styles of the Greats.*
"Jack popularized the terms 'attack,' 'the big game' and
'percentage tennis.' There were many attacking players
before Kramer but none who consistently came in behind
every serve. The big serve combined with the big volley
became known as the Big Game. The words 'percentage
tennis' described a theory of play that included such
Kramerisms as hitting every forehand approach shot
down the line, serving at three-quarter speed to the backhand on important points, and coasting on the opponent's delivery until the opportunity came for the break."

The idea of turning tennis into a geometrical theory
was taken to Kramer by an automotive engineer, Clifton
Roche, a tennis buff who contacted Kramer when Jake
was a rising star in his late teens at a club in Beverly Hills.
Partly, it consisted of the mathematical unsoundness of
hitting the ball to certain spots in certain situations. For

instance, when running to the left sideline the player should never return the ball down that sideline because it gave the opponent too big an angle for a crosscourt return. Roche had worked out theories for almost any shot from almost any spot.

Mercer Beasley, who coached Ellsworth Vines and Frank Parker among other stars, had developed fundamental theories of a similar nature in the 1930s. He had likened a player's half of the court to an area controlled by traffic lights. Since returning a ball from behind the baseline is unlikely to produce an outright winner, the risks of hitting a hard shot or one aimed at the baseline are outweighed by the dangers of an error. Hence, in this "red" zone, a player should merely keep the ball in play, waiting for a better opportunity as the rally ensues.

The area between the baseline and the service line is less dangerous. Accordingly, depending upon the situation, a player can be more aggressive in this "amber" zone, perhaps even hit winners. But, obviously, the best place to hammer hard shots or to angle for the lines is the area between the service line and the net, and it is in this "green" haven that the attacking player can go all out.

Roche moved on from this Mercer philosophy to incorporate theories of angles that increased Kramer's chances of gaining superior court position and holding it. On the serve, he favored placement over power. By placing the ball into the far corner he could swing an opponent wide of the court, shortening the angle of return. Kramer, at the net, then could volley deep to the other corner for a winner or set up a return so weak he could put it away.

He varied his serve according to the score. If he were ahead 40–15, say, he might try for an ace down the middle. But at 30–40 or 40–30 he'd hit the percentage shot; move his opponent wide with the serve to the far corner. And, of course, Kramer was no fancy Dan; he could hit power with the best of hitters and this, combined with his use of angles and "traffic lights," made him nearly unbeatable.

Kramer played all games as a kid growing up in Las Vegas, where he was born August 1, 1921, and in San Bernardino, near Los Angeles, where his father David was a Union Pacific railroad engineer. At fourteen he was taken into the Southern California Tennis Association's junior development program under director Perry Jones, an elegant, powerful tennis figure who was influential in the development of scores of glittering kids—Vines, Budge, Gonzales, Mo Connolly, even Helen Wills of an earlier era.

Jones arranged a tennis membership for Kramer at the fashionable Los Angeles Tennis Club, and each day the boy took a ninety-minute streetcar ride to Beverly Hills for a tennis lesson from the pro there, Dick Skeen. Then Jones set up young Jake for three sessions a week with Ellsworth Vines whose style he endeavored to ape over the next five months. Such concentrated work brought on so swift a development that in 1935, as an unseeded player, Kramer won the national boys' singles and two years later the national interscholastic championship. Though he had just turned sixteen that fall, he went into the nationals at Forest Hills and, quite properly, was knocked off in an early round. A year later, however, he'd climbed to No. 15 in the national rankings and the year after that, in 1939, he was chosen as a Davis Cupper against Australia at Philadelphia. He was then the youngest player, at seventeen years ten months and thirty days, ever to play in the challenge round, a record until John Alexander played for Australia in 1968, five months and two days younger. Then along came Bjorn Borg for Sweden in 1972 at age fifteen.

Kramer's appearance in Davis Cup doubles, partnered by another down-cheeked youth, Joe Hunt, came at the whim of Walter Pate, the team captain who a few years earlier had boldly inserted young Don Budge into the American lineup to wrest the Cup from Britain. This time, Pate over-reached, for the Kramer–Hunt combination was no match for Australia's Jack Bromwich and Adrian Quist, who lost only one set. Since singles players Bobby Riggs and Frank Parker were also scuttled by the Aussies and since 1939 was the year Hitler decided to take over the world, the Australians thus harbored the trophy for six years: Davis Cup play was abandoned until 1946 while Australia, Britain, and other Commonwealth countries were heavily involved in a war, as were all the overrun countries of Europe.

Kramer played tennis for three more years before going into the U.S. Coast Guard. He and his buddy Ted Schroeder, eleven days his senior, won twelve doubles championships in fifteen tournaments in 1940, including Forest Hills where, at nineteen, they were the youngest pair to win that title. That winter Kramer, who had climbed to No. 6 in singles rankings, took a scholarship at Rollins College in Winter Park, Florida, to keep his game sharp. He toured South America in 1941, won the national doubles at home again with Schroeder and in 1942 became very close to the best player in America when he won ten straight singles crowns. But he missed the nationals, felled by appendicitis, and Schroeder won it.

Though Kramer had gone into the Coast Guard late in 1942, it appeared that 1943 would still be his year on the courts since he was able to continue playing. He won the Pacific Southwest crown, regained with Schroeder the U.S. doubles title his appendix had cost them a year earlier, but then was foiled again in the singles when he was laid low by ptomaine poisoning on the eve of the final and by Lt. Joe Hunt in the match itself. Hunt was a fine young emerging player, ranked first in the U.S. that year of 1943 but deprived of his proper place in the game's lore by the war. He was a naval lieutenant killed in action in the South Pacific.

Early in 1944 just before he, too, embarked for the South Pacific, Kramer made one last wartime tennis appearance. He was matched with Don Budge in a Red Cross charity event and, surprisingly, whipped the professional star 6–3, 6–2. He commanded a naval LST in five invasions through the next two years, including those of New Guinea and the Philippines, and four months after his discharge in January 1946 he beat national champion Frank Parker in straight sets in a Southern California tournament to celebrate his return to tennis. He rushed off to Wimbledon and appeared headed for the championship there even while developing large watery blisters that he endeavored to minimize by covering them with bandages, tape, and a special glove, But the clever

Drobny blocked his path with an assortment of left-handed power and precision in a two and a half hour match.

Yet Kramer, characteristically, turned this defeat to advantage in the long run, remarking later that whenever he was in a tough spot he simply called to mind the pain he'd felt and the frustration the Czech had forced on him, and recognized that things weren't as bad now as they'd been then.

Back home in California after the Wimbledon defeat he allowed his hands to heal, conditioned them slowly in the recovery stage, developed callouses, and beat everybody in sight. That included Bob Falkenburg with loss of a mere eight games in the Forest Hills semifinals and, in the final, another Californian, Tom Brown, who'd been the tournament's upset specialist and, indeed, Kramer's partner in the doubles conquest at Wimbledon a few months earlier. Brown had eliminated U.S. defending champion Frankie Parker in the quarterfinals and the star of the eastern grass-court circuit, Gardnar Mulloy, in the semis. After a slam, bam, wham first set in which Kramer narrowly prevailed in the sixteenth game to pull out a 9–7 edge, Big Jake toyed with Tom in the next pair, 6–3 and 6–0. That made Kramer, at long last, No. 1, and he endorsed the ranking in December's Davis Cup confrontation in Sydney by nailing Jack Bromwich and Dinny Pails in singles and teaming with Schroeder to avenge the hiding he and Joe Hunt had taken from Bromwich and Adrian Quist in doubles many long years ago, back there when he was seventeen before the war.

Now Kramer knew he was on his way to a fortune to

accompany his fame but he recognized that to acquire the fortune he needed to win Wimbledon and repeat at Forest Hills in 1947, proving he could handle the persistent Drobny and the stubborn Parker. The draw did not permit him to test his skills against that pair at Wimbledon; he contented himself with demolishing poor Tom Brown again, requiring a minimum forty-five minutes as King George VI applauded warmly during the match and shook his hand affably after it.

The Wimbledon win and the royal handshake were only enjoyable interludes in Kramer's quest, however. The day after, the determined young man, now twenty-six, flew to Chicago and the home of Bob Harman, a noted coach and instruction-book author. Kramer felt his forehand had not been infallible at Wimbledon. He believed, too, that Frank Parker's forehand owned chinks. So he reasoned that if he were going to beat Parker at Forest Hills the way to do it was to outgun him with cross-court forehands. To help him accomplish this, he paid Harman for a series of lessons designed to consolidate his forehand.

Everything worked out as he'd plotted. He found Drobny in his half of the draw, meaning they'd meet in the semifinal if both survived that far, and Parker heading the seeds in the other half, meaning the collision in the final was perfectly possible. When he met Drobny he got even for the previous year's Wimbledon setback, rifling his new solid forehand to punch holes in the Czech's left-handed backhand and beat him in straight sets. That moved him into the final round where, sure enough, Parker awaited him. Calling again on the new solidity his work with the Chicago instructor Harman had given him, Big Jake wore down Parker's forehand remorselessly and claimed his second national singles crown in a row.

There was nothing left for him now but the pros; he'd clearly established his mastery of every amateur. Promoter Jack Harris was anxious to add this fresh new face because Don Budge had been dissolved as a gate attraction by the tiny extrovert Bobby Riggs. Thus, Kramer and Riggs were clearly established as the two best tennis players in the world and, in Riggs' mind at least, there was no question as to the order. "I can beat Jack Kramer on grass, on clay, on cement, indoors or outdoors," Riggs said, goading the inventor of the Big Game.

Kramer really needed small goading beyond a guarantee from promoter Harris of a minimum $50,000 to tour with Riggs. The opening match was booked for Madison Square Garden on the night after Christmas in 1947. But on Christmas night snow began to fall upon New York and by mid-afternoon on Boxing Day fifteen inches had drifted down and more was falling. Peering from a window in the Lexington Hotel, Harris bemoaned his luck, convinced the weatherman was concocting a cruel post-Christmas turkey. At 7 o'clock he and Kramer and Riggs set off from the Lexington through streets knee-deep in snow. There was no traffic. Everything was at a snow enshrouded standstill. Occasional abandoned cars sat whitely silent at curbs. Nothing on the surface moved except the glum and silent trio pushing through the snow toward the Garden.

When they arrived, the preliminary players, Aussie Dinny Pails and the bow-legged Pancho Segura, were already going through the motions of a one-set singles en-

counter before a near-empty house. By 9 o'clock the snow
was no longer falling and, surprisingly, the Garden was
beginning to fill. People fresh from the subways or snow-
covered and laughing and carrying snowshoes came
charging into the Garden from the outdoors where
twenty-six inches of snow had fallen. The suddenly be-
sieged box office reissued tickets to people who had been
unable to go home to pick them up but who called to get
the numbers. By match-time more than 15,000 were
turning what had loomed as a financial disaster into a
slaphappy adventure for themselves and a take of
$55,730.50 for the delighted Harris.

And on the court, Riggs lived up to his promises. An
experienced pro with deceptively hard shots and uncanny
anticipation, he kept the nervous Kramer off stride with
his assortment of junk and beat him 6–2, 10–8, 4–6, 6–4,
and repeated the dosage two nights later in Pittsburgh.
But after that, Kramer settled into his own game, his percentage game with the big serve and volley and in succeeding matches he subdued the resolute but over-
matched Riggs by sixty-nine matches to twenty. The
eighty-nine stops on the tour produced a gross of
$248,000. Kramer's arrangement with Harris, the pro-
moter, was that he'd receive a minimum of $50,000 or
thirty-five percent of the gross. Thus, the tour was worth
better than $85,000 to Kramer.

Riggs and Harris had a falling out before a new season
was launched. Riggs stepped in as the promoter, hoping
to lure Kramer's old partner Ted Schroeder from the
amateurs, but Schroeder declined. So Riggs turned to a
new young star, Pancho Gonzales, who had won the U.S.
singles title in 1948 and 1949, but Gonzales was only

twenty-one and his burgeoning game was no match for the established cannons Kramer was mustering. Kramer was merciless, whipping the rookie in 96 of their 123 matches.

A couple of years later Riggs tried coeducational tours on the public. He signed Gorgeous Gussy Moran, the rage of Wimbledon, and the cool slender Pauline Betz to travel with Kramer and Pancho Segura, the popular and colorful Equador export. Moran was close to being the most publicized player in the game. She had shocked the old twits of Wimbledon by wearing provocative lace-embroidered panties there. Her game was no hell but Gussie was an eyeful in an era before it became uncouth for men to appreciate publicly a lady's lovely lines. The problem was that she couldn't beat Betz and Segura was no match for Kramer so after a ninety-two stop tour Riggs had no one to send anywhere.

Into this breach stepped Kramer in a new role: he took over as not just the star attraction but also as the promoter, and the way he retained the public's attention year after year was simply to go around breaking up championship Davis Cup teams. And he did this by offering guaranteed minimums that the Davis Cup stars found impossible to reject. When Australia won the international trophy in 1952 Kramer deprived the Aussies of their kingpin, Frank Sedgman, by guaranteeing him $75,000 and promising thirty percent of the total receipts if that figure were higher. Then he proceeded to knock off Sedgman by fifty-four matches to forty-one. When Tony Trabert later led the U.S. in regaining the Cup, Kramer was there with the fat check and the tall percentage to nail down Trabert. Similarly, little Ken Rosewall.

By the mid-1950s Kramer was promoting a different kind of professional tour. He had built up so formidable a stable of tough young pros that instead of touring with a handful on one-night stands he began travelling with them all for round-robin tournaments in major centers. Each year, too, he took pen and contract to every emerging amateur star, deploring the under-the-table payoffs of amateur tennis and extolling the above-board unhypocritical payoffs of the pros.

Kramer's own integrity went up against one of its stiffest tests in England in 1957 just after he had guaranteed the newest Australian sensation, Lew Hoad, an unprecedented $125,000. Obviously, Hoad was a man Kramer planned to hang his promotional hat on. Yet, as luck would have it, Kramer and Hoad were drawn to face each other in the first round at Wembley on London's outskirts. Now if Kramer were to wallop his newest star in his professional debut the result could only dampen gate receipts in subsequent appearances by the gifted Hoad, particularly since Kramer was now thirty-six years old and obviously on the shady side of the mountain. Yet Kramer went after his young Aussie attraction with guns blazing, rushing the net behind his calculated serve, cannily playing his percentage game. He whipped him, and when it was over he cursed himself. "Dammit to hell," he grated to his friend C. M. Jones, the editor of the British magazine *Lawn Tennis*, "there's only one way I know how to play this game, and that's to win. I don't know how much tonight will cost me, but I'll bet it's a ton."

That was Kramer's last year as a player. He pitted Hoad against the newcomer Pancho Gonzales, whom he'd signed to a seven-year contract, on a tour of eighty-seven cities on three continents and although Hoad got off to an eighteen-to-nine advantage in the early stages, Gonzales then went on to wallop him in fifty-one matches. To keep the pot boiling, Kramer pursued Australia's clever Davis Cup duo of Mal Anderson and Ashley Cooper even before the Cup final of 1958. And then he got himself involved in yet another dichotomy situation. Anxious that Anderson and Cooper should distinguish themselves in the Challenge Round to enhance their attractiveness when they turned pro, Kramer nonetheless acceded to a request from his old friend and U.S. Davis Cup team captain Perry Jones to coach the American team. He did such a successful job in bringing the game of Alex Olmedo to its peak that Olmedo almost single-handedly produced an American victory over Kramer's pair of Aussie recruits. He always knew only one way to go and that was all out.

By 1960 the round-robin tourists included the tennis firmament's top attractions—Gonzales, Segura, Rosewall, Anderson, Cooper, Trabert, Olmeda—and while Kramer preached his gospel of open tennis the pros often bickered among themselves over the contracts and percentage arrangements they'd made with promoter Kramer. So that year Big Jake forsook promotional reins and left operation of the tour to an association of the players.

"I felt my presence in the movement might be detrimental to the pro game," he said. "It was necessary that the pros work in harmony with the amateur associations. I didn't want to be a stumbling block."

He continued talking out against the hypocrisy of amateur tennis, appealing for open tournaments. He continued his association with the Wilson company whose racquets and equipment he endorsed and promoted, and he turned to a commentator's role as television networks began turning their cameras on the evolving game. When open tennis finally arrived in 1968, no one had done more to bring it into a new and enormously popular public spotlight than Big Jake, Jack Kramer.

Pancho Gonzales

PANCHO GONZALES

[1928–   ]

ＰANCHO GONZALES was not an easy man to like until a
time when long streaks of gray were finding their way
into the thick lion's mane that crowned his scowling features. After that he came very close to being an American
folk hero.

"He was ungracious to say the least, a loner, and an
absolute jerk on the court," Rod Laver wrote of the Gonzales he met across the net when first he turned professional. "He tried to take every advantage."

But later, as Gonzales entered his forties and still
played tennis with a kind of majestic aloofness, a daunt-
less competitiveness, Laver, too, began to see him in a
new and different light. "I was finding myself enthralled
to watch him, just like any other spectator."

Whatever the difference was it was in the eye of the
beholder, for Gonzales never changed in style or demeanor once he set foot on a tennis court. In his teens or
in his forties or at any age between, his only concern was
that he be the player who fired the final successful shot in
any match.

In his passion for his craft Gonzales was not unlike the
Boston Red Sox slugger Ted Williams, a parallel plucked
by Richard Schickel in *The World of Tennis.* "There was a

ferocious purity in his commitment to the game itself that was, finally, awesome—analogous in a way to that of Ted Williams's similarly fierce commitment to the essence of his chosen sport."

Gonzales smoldered and fumed, off the court and on. He railed against the game's officials during the brief period when he was an amateur, and he sullenly refused to speak to the pro tour promoter Jack Kramer after Kramer signed him to a contract at what Gonzales belatedly decided was outrageously low reward. He seethed on the court, often at himself if his shots were missing, and at linesmen and spectators, too. Once, at Wimbledon, he hurled his racquet at the umpire's chair and stomped from the court in a fury, and another time he went into the stands in a vain effort to lay hands on a raucous heckler. "Pancho is very even-tempered," a friend observed of him one time. "He's always mad."

But, in the end, his uncompromising dedication to his game, his vast skills, his palpable enthrallment with the task and, not to be overlooked, his advancing years combined to elicit a sentimental response in the public that elevated him to a cool pedestal in the lore of the games people play and rhapsodize about.

Perhaps the moment that brought about this metamorphosis was reached at Wimbledon in 1969 when he engaged the flashing twenty-five-year-old Charlie Pasarell, sixteen years his junior, in what was and always will be the longest tournament match in that hoary old greensward's history. Pasarell was an American Davis Cupper at his peak then, a man with a serve for the angels and a strong all-round game. He had whipped the defending champion Manuel Santana in 1967 and, a year later, had gone five sets with the No. 2 seed, Australia's Ken Rosewall. In their record confrontation, he and Gonzales played 112 games that demanded five hours and twelve minutes spread over two days when darkness overtook them after two sets.

Rain had washed out play on the preceding day and damp courts had kept the players fretful until six o'clock in the evening for the first game in this match in the round of sixteen. Pasarell took it and held it and went right on holding his service for more than two hours. Ordinarily, such consistency would have assured consummate victory, except that until the forty-sixth game the old lion didn't lose his service either. Then, with the light waning, Pasarell, at long and exhaustive last and leading by 23–22, broke Gonzales to win the first set.

In the twilight the weary Pancho began collecting his racquets at the sidelines, hopeful that he'd be more fortunate when play resumed the next day. The number of games was comparable to a match with scores of, say, 7–5, 9–7, 10–8, a real brute, and Gonzales aimed his weary bones toward a long hot shower. But wait! The umpire, Mike Gibson, was directing that play continue, that the second set be undertaken. Vainly, Gonzales appealed for an overnight suspension of the marathon. But in Gibson's view the light was entirely adequate for a resumption.

Fuming and petulant, Gonzales went back to the baseline after three appeals and, typically, stomped through the motions, steaming and muttering. The undismayed Pasarell whistled through the second set at 6–1, and when Gibson now called for an adjournment and stepped down from his chair Gonzales sent his racquet crashing against the barely deserted perch. Gibson ignored him, the crowd set up a mild chorus of boos, and Gonzales raged from the court. Then he stayed up well past midnight playing cards in the locker room while Pasarell retired early to be ready for next day's resumption.

In a remarkable revelation of stamina, Gonzales picked up the match where he'd left it after the opening set, matching Pasarell game for game in another collision of big serves. As he'd done in the first set, Pasarell lobbed whenever Gonzales approached the net and dropped short shots when he played deep, running the older man to tire him. But never breaking him. Indeed, this time it was Pasarell who finally yielded a service break, and Gonzales, winning the crowd to him as he prowled the court relentlessly, refusing to yield, stayed alive at 16–14. And the crowd kept growing as word spread of the old lion's stubborn struggle.

In the fourth set with Gonzales leading 4–3, Pasarell slipped again, double-faulting on game point and setting up Gonzales to win the set if he could hold service. With lavish disdain for the pressure of this moment, Pancho rifled his cannonballs as though engaged in a practice session and ran out the set at 6–3.

Now, incredibly, he was dead even. The stands had become completely populated and interest in Pancho's astonishing climb had even attracted hundreds to an electric scoreboard outside the court that registered each point and extracted roars each time the old man lit the board.

After nine games of what had become the longest match in Wimbledon history, the end was in sight. Gonzales was trailing 4–5 and though he was serving he was simply too weary to hold off the fresher man. He dropped the first three points of his service and Pasarell, ahead 40–0, held three match points. He lifted a towering lob, compelling Gonzales to undertake yet another draining overhead smash, but Pancho refused to play it safe, refused to back off the challenge. He crashed a cross-court bullet that made it 15–40. Next, poised at the net, he lunged for a Pasarell passing shot and volleyed it off the tape for another point—30–40. Next, a vicious serve that Pasarell couldn't handle. Deuce! Reprieved, Pancho banged off two more points and saved the match at 5–5.

Still, it was only a reprieve, not a pardon. Pasarell pushed ahead 6–5 and got another match point on Gonzales's serve. Pancho held. Then 7–6 and then two more match points. Pancho held. Then 8–7 and then another match point, the seventh, and somehow Gonzales held again. And then, with the fans really not believing what they were seeing and the score knotted at 9–9, Gonzales broke Pasarell to go ahead for the first time in a marathon that now had reached 111 games. For the first time, it was Pasarell who had to hold or fold. Just to make an unbelievable story ludicrous, Gonzales served out the 112th game *at love*.

Luckily, some semblance of sanity or at least of reality was preserved two days later when Pancho was knocked out in the quarterfinal round, and the two renowned Australians Rod Laver and John Newcombe went eventually into Wimbledon's final, with Laver winning his fourth championship at the famous old shrine.

Indeed, great as he was for two full decades, Gonzales never did win at Wimbledon, but this was more the fault of the game's hypocrisy in the 1950s and 1960s than Pancho's. By the time open tennis arrived in 1968 Pancho had been a professional beating everybody in sight for nineteen years. While the amateurs were taking their money under the table, he was grabbing checks in public but of course being prevented from picking up any of them among the soiled purebreds at Forest Hills, Wimbledon, Roland Garros or any of the other holier-than-thou temples of the time.

Gonzales turned pro as an impulsive immature young man of twenty-one, a Mexican-American born in Los Angeles, raised during the Depression, the eldest in a family of seven whose father was a housepainter. When Pancho was seven, playing in the streets, the left side of his face was ripped open in a car crash, and all his life that scar turned crimson during periods of high excitement or strenuous activity. He was named Richard Alonzo Gonzales when he was born on May 9, 1928, and nicknamed Pancho as a kid in school. There were no silver spoons in the household.

"Food wasn't abundant," he said once, "but it was filling enough and we never went hungry. Our clothes were just clothes, inexpensive but clean. We wished for many things that never came."

Remarkably, he never had a tennis lesson, not as a youngster and not as a teen-ager when his game began to burgeon. Still, tennis possibly kept him out of serious trouble because as a poor and energetic kid he bounded endlessly across the public courts of Exposition Park amid the smells of hot dogs and frying onions while his peers were out stealing hubcaps, or whatever. His mother bought him a cheap racquet when he was twelve, hoping to keep him from joining the wild ones. In a sense, she was too successful; his devotion not only kept him out of

pool rooms but out of classrooms, as well. His ability attracted the attention of the area tennis czar Perry Jones
but when Pancho refused to go to school except when
rain kept him off the courts Jones refused to let him play
against the other prize juniors in his stable.

Yet nothing could prevent young Gonzales from playing *somebody*, and he flailed away day after day at Exposition Park against anyone who could swing a racquet. He
grew tall in his late teens, stretching to six-feet-three and
eventually filling out to a tough 185 pounds. He became a
handsome kid, too, with long swarthy features, a smol-
dering expression, and black challenging eyes.

Scorned by Jones, he nonetheless played every tournament for which he was eligible and when he was nineteen he reached the final round of the Southern California championships. There, he was opposed by Herbie
Flam, the national junior champion two years earlier who
had already tasted the fruits of recognition on the eastern
grass-court circuit. In what was to become a pattern of his
play, he lost the first set 10–8 and trailed 5–6 and 0–40 as
he served with three match points against him. In this
crucible he did what he was to do so many times in the
years to come: he served three successive aces to deadlock
the set, went on to win it at 8–6 and then won the deciding set 6–4. He accepted the championship wearing
clothes his mother had bought for him so that he
wouldn't play at the elegant Los Angeles Tennis Club
looking shabby: white running shoes for a dollar, a fifty-
nine cent white shirt, and white shorts at a dollar-fifty.

Two months later he was at Forest Hills in the nationals, survivor of a first-round match. Then he was
drawn against rising Davis Cupper Gardnar Mulloy and

he took Mulloy to five sets before departing. Later, in the Pacific Southwest event he disposed of internationalist Jaroslav Drobny, Bob Falkenburg and Frankie Parker before being sidelined by Ted Schroeder. He was definitely on his way, this untutored Chicano.

When he got to Forest Hills in 1948 he was seeded No. 8 among most of the world's best amateurs, though the field did not include Schroeder or the defending champion Jack Kramer who had turned professional. Falkenburg, who had won Wimbledon, was there, and so were Parker, Mulloy, Drobny, and the rest, making Gonzales, four months past twenty, just another outsider. In spite of Falkenburg's Wimbledon win, Parker was No. 1 in the seedings, and Gonzales, piling through three matches, met him in the quarterfinals. Surprisingly, he handled him in four sets. Next was the clever left-hander Drobny who got off to a 10–8 win in the first set and sped ahead in the second. Gonzales, who seemed to revel in marathons in the era before the tiebreaker terminated them, finally solved the Czech's wily game halfway through that second set and pulled it out at 11–9. Then he waltzed, 6–0 and 6–3, and that took him to the final round against another lightly regarded pre-tournament nobody, the South African Eric Sturgess, who soon was anonymous again; Pancho polished him off in straight sets, although not without injecting one of his patented marathons—a 14–12 margin in the third.

Curiously, he now slipped into a long decline. Ted Schroeder, who many thought would succeed his Davis Cup doubles partner Kramer when Big Jake turned pro but who had not competed at Forest Hills, potted him soundly in the Pacific Southwest event, and in succeeding tournaments Gonzales frequently did not survive even to the round of sixteen. So persistent was the slide that his Forest Hills triumph began to appear a fluke and he took on the aroma of a cheese champion. Indeed, he even picked up another nickname—Gorgo, for gorgonzola.

What appears to have happened, though tennis historians are vague on this, is that Gonzales took to loafing and enjoying a life that for twenty years had been blessed with few of the normal pleasures, for when he turned up at the national indoor championships in April 1949 he was fifteen pounds overweight. Nevertheless, he struggled and sweated to his first tournament victory since Forest Hills in this one, and then added the national clay-court championships. His reputation still carried holes, though, because the fields weren't particularly strong in either of these events, and he still hadn't proved he could handle Schroeder.

Inevitably, however, their paths crossed in the national championships at Forest Hills that fall when the cheese champion had to establish whether he was a worthy title-holder or just another one-time Charlie, and the stage was set in the purest light when both emerged as finalists.

Excitement had been building for months for this matchup, and as each made his way through the draw it continued to climb. The blond outgoing Schroeder seemed the logical heir to Kramer's position as the No. 1 amateur; he had been a crowd-pleasing partner to Big Jake in their Davis Cup triumphs and he had won Wimbledon's singles that summer. Still, the dark and glowering Gonzales *was* the defending champion, however cheesy, and he had a following, too.

So when they met in the concrete horseshoe of Forest

Hills, enormous tension had already preceded them to the center court. And all through the first set it built ever higher as the players matched service through thirty-three games. But then Gonzales fell behind 0–40 as he tried to make it 17–17. He responded to the challenge with three blistering serves for deuce, fell back again on a net-cord shot by Schroeder. On the next serve, Gonzales followed to the net and laid down a volley that he and many of the spectators believed caught the line. But the linesman saw it otherwise, called the ball out, and Schroeder had the set at 18–16. Quickly, as Gonzales brooded over the call, Schroeder piled up a commanding lead in the second set, kept the pressure on, and ran it out at 6–2.

Pancho's spirits took a typical flip-flop in this predicament and he brought his game to a higher level. Undaunted by his deficit he lost a mere three games in the next two sets, and though Schroeder fought steadfastly in the fifth and was even after eight games he could not maintain the pace. Gonzales took the next two games for the match, and now in this repeat performance if he were still a cheese champion it was purest Camembert. To make it stick, he beat Schroeder in the Pacific Southwest, and there was no longer any question as to who was No. 1.

Though he'd proved himself, Gonzales was still a long way from being an experienced player. Less than two years prior to his Forest Hills triumph he'd been that unknown kid in the fifty-nine cent shirt in the Southern California championships. Internationally, he'd played a mere two singles matches in Davis Cup competition, winning both that year of 1949, and what he needed now was a settling-in period, and perhaps a run at Roland Garros and Wimbledon.

Instead, he found himself on an airplane heading home to Los Angeles one dark night seated beside, by the sheerest coincidence, Bobby Riggs. Riggs had turned promoter, and had planned matching Jack Kramer and Ted Schroeder in the 1950 tour. But Schroeder had backed off, and at Kramer's suggestion Riggs had decided to go after young Gonzales. Such a coincidence, finding him on the same plane! By the time they'd landed in L.A., Riggs had Gonzales's name on a contract—$60,000 or thirty percent of the gate, whichever was larger.

As it turned out, Gonzales made a very welcome $75,000 duelling with the professional king Kramer, but he'd also painted himself into a desperate corner. He was simply no match for the powerful Kramer's vast court know-how in an exhaustive tour of 123 matches. Pancho won a mere twenty-seven, and in the cutthroat professional game of the time there was no room for second-best. He was dead at the box office and, of course, his amateur future was all behind him. He had no place to turn but the tennis shop at Exposition Park where he wiled away his hours stringing racquets and playing occasional exhibitions, a forgotten former champion. His savings dwindled, he separated from his wife Henrietta, and he turned to hot-rod racing, poker, and even bowling to get his mind out of its despond. He survived in this manner for four listless years.

Out of the blue in 1955 came the voice of the man who'd sent him into oblivion—Kramer. Did he want to tour in a round-robin series of matches with Pancho Segura and Frank Sedgman? Did he!

In spite of the long layoff, he was a match for them. But his success seemed only a stop-gap, for Kramer was pursuing two red-hot young Aussies, Lew Hoad and Ken Rosewall, for the 1956 tour. Then at the last moment they changed their minds, pulled out of their verbal commitment, and left Kramer high and dry with the Wimbledon and Forest Hills champion, America's Tony Trabert, whom he had signed at a $75,000 guarantee. Kramer had nowhere to turn but to Gonzales if there were to be any tour at all, but Gonzales was unaware of Big Jake's tight predicament. Accordingly, Pancho was insulted when Kramer offered him a flat $15,000 to tour with Trabert, but he had to forego his wounded pride if he were to continue to eat. He agreed. He shattered Trabert in a 101-match tour, winning 74 times, and in succeeding years he hammered Hoad and Rosewall and, later, even the masterful Laver in a one-man assault on Australian giants.

He refused all conversation with Kramer, whom he felt had taken scandalous advantage of him, though he continued to play a grim and silent gin rummy game with him. It was in this period that Laver described him as a jerk. He travelled alone in souped-up sports cars, vroom-vrooming across the landscape in the dark of night, and avoiding all but the most necessary social contact with his opponents. Still, as Schickel notes in *The World of Tennis,* "his lonely trail made him, for people who really cared about tennis, a legendary figure of heroic proportions."

There developed, too, during these years, a glowing illustration of Pancho's dedication to his game. It was revealed in his tour against Lew Hoad, the skilled and resourceful Australian who'd won Wimbledon's singles back to back in 1956 and 1957. Early in their tour Gonzales trailed by eighteen to nine, largely because Hoad had detected a flaw in Pancho's powerful groundstrokes. Because of a restriction in his self-taught grip, Hoad noted, Gonzales was unable to hit a crosscourt backhand shot when he was driven deep to a corner. Every return was hit down the line. Recognizing this, Hoad was always there at the alley to volley a winner.

Sensing this, Gonzales made a fundamental alteration in his grip, a towering accomplishment against a top-flight opponent, switching from the bunched-finger grip he'd used all his life to an open-finger hold that provided more flexibility and enabled him to fire the ball crosscourt.

"Before long he was passing me with his backhand," Hoad said later. "Only a colossal natural player could have done it."

Gonzales, restored to the heights and assuredly the master of the professionals, began to talk of winding down his career in his mid-thirties, becoming a resident pro in Las Vegas and a frequent television commentator. But with each retirement he would unretire, a fire-horse hearing the clang of bells. In May 1964 after only one tournament in three years he turned up at the U.S. Professional Indoor tournament and on successive nights beat Laver, Hoad, and Rosewall. Two years later, after another retirement, he went to Wembley, outside London, for the World Professional Championship, knocked out Rosewall in a sizzling semifinal and then beat Laver, who was reaching the peak of his wondrous game by then, in a glowing final.

By 1969 and at forty-one, Pancho was announcing a

retirement after almost every tournament, particularly in the wake of the marathon with Pasarell, but in October that year in the $50,000 Tournament of Champions at Las Vegas, the old lion, now an American institution, hamstrung Arthur Ashe in the final, 6–0, 6–2, 6–4. That, he said, was positively his last tournament. A year later, there he was in Madison Square Garden for the inaugural of a new world series of tennis, a $10,000 winner-take-all match with Laver. There were 18,000 people jammed around the court in the big arena and there was no question which player was in their hearts. They had gone there remembering the old champ nostalgically but they stayed to cheer his skills as he shaded the Aussie lefthander.

And still he wasn't through. In 1971, amazingly, he won the Pacific Southwest tournament, roping a field that included the new upstart Jimmy Connors. That should have been enough, but even in his mid-forties Pancho was venturing out of the Las Vegas woodwork occasionally to drive wild men wilder for a set or two, a full-blown legend in his own time.

ROD LAVER

[1938–   ]

𝓑ECAUSE ROD LAVER dominated the world's tennis courts so completely through most of the 1960s and was still such an enormously effective figure on them well into the 1970s, the notion arises that he was one of those rare and gifted birds to whom excellence comes as easily as breathing—that he was, in short, a natural.

How else could a runt of five-feet-seven and 145 pounds, a scrawny, sunken-chested, bandy-legged, unstylish, and thoroughly unathletic-looking fellow who had even been known to wear damp *cabbage leaves* on his head under a floppy brimmed hat ever ascend to that mantle reserved for such giants as Tilden and Budge and Kramer unless he were plugged into some sort of divine pipeline?

For here was the only player in tennis history to win the Grand Slam as an amateur and repeat the feat as a professional after open tennis joined all of the world's best players. Here was the man who, in 1969, won the Australian Open in the 105-degree heat of January, the French Open on the slow debilitating red clay of Paris in the spring, Wimbledon on the manicured lawns of England in mid-summer, the U.S. Open on the scuffed grass—"a bloody cow pasture most of the time"—of

Rod Laver

Forest Hills in September, and, between times, the South African Championship, the British Indoor, the U.S. Pro, and eleven other professional championships, a total of eighteen titles in thirty-three tournaments all over the world.

And yet Rod Laver was nothing like a born champion. As a youngster within the narrow confines of his own family of three boys, he was ranked No. 3. As an amateur he lost his first two Davis Cup matches in 1959. He was knocked out at Wimbledon in his first two tries in 1959 and 1960. He dropped successive straight-set matches to fellow-countrymen Neale Fraser and Roy Emerson at Forest Hills in 1960 and 1961. He did win the Australian Championship twice, in 1960 and 1962, but that hardly compares with Emerson's six triumphs there. And then when he turned professional in 1963 he was whipped humiliatingly in tours by Lew Hoad and Ken Rosewall.

But after that—look out! For almost a decade, there was nobody anywhere who could match strokes for long with Rod Laver.

How come? How come that this little red-haired freckle-faced knobby-kneed *squirt,* whom the mentor, slave driver, and David Cup captain Harry Hopman dubbed Rocket in a disparaging quip—"I called him the Rocket because he wasn't"—how come he learned to wield a tennis racquet like some sort of d'Artagnan flashing a sword?

Viewed from the right side in profile, Laver looked like a man who couldn't lick his lips. But from the *left* side, here was the essence of a champion. "It's the *arm,*" the Canadian writer Earl McRae said of him once. "The arm is startling. It is huge. A deformity. If Laver weighs 145, then 100 of it is in the arm. He's an extension of the arm. Somebody took the arm once and measured it. The forearm was twelve inches. The wrist was seven inches. The forearm was bigger than Rocky Marciano's and the wrist was bigger than Floyd Patterson's, both of them former world's heavyweight boxing champions."

While the left arm was the instrument that delivered the *coup de grace* when Laver ruled as the undisputed king of the courts, this left arm that dwarfed his right and that he developed by squeezing a tennis ball in every waking hour when he wasn't on the court, he had other vital attributes. Attributes such as a palpable determination, magnificent physical condition, unswerving concentration, and a well nigh relentless dedication. He was a stoic who played in pain, a man whose temperament was impervious to such distractions as bad calls, ranting opponents, flukey shots, and crowd noises.

He once said that the hardest part of the game to maintain was concentration. "You can have all the shots but if you don't have concentration, you'll never be a champion," he noted, citing the American star of the 1960s, Dennis Ralston, and the rude Rumanian Ilie Nastase for illustration. "Ralston's a good player but he'll sometimes lose two or three games he should have won because he gets distracted too easily. Nastase's good, too, but you've seen him throw tantrums on the court. That's bushleague in my book. He hasn't grown up. There's no need for it. Concentration comes with experience, maturity. You must think only of the ball. You wipe out the crowd, the noises. Just the ball. Never take your eye off the ball. Think of that ball all the time. Getting it back. If you lose a point, forget it. It's gone. Get the next one. If a linesman calls a ball out and you *know* it was good, what can you do? Nothing. Only aggravate yourself. So, again, forget it. Get the next one."

With Laver, the game was the thing. He had no time nor patience for the "hot dogs," the players like Nastase and Pancho Gonzales who carried histrionics to the heavens. He never tried to psyche out an opponent, only to outstroke him. "Nothing mental with me," he reflected once. "I do it by physically beating him. I return everything he has, his best shots. That upsets him. Of course, I never give him a shot he likes. You get to know what shots he plays best, whoever he is. Know his weakness and work on it. The mental follows the physical. I go hard for the first point of the game and the first two games of the set. If you get the first service break, it's psychologically upsetting. Always *look* like a winner. Think positive. Don't lose your composure. I usually brush my teeth if it's a big match. Shave, comb my hair, whiten my shoes. Never let an opponent know you're tired. When I change ends I walk briskly, head up. If he's gasping, he thinks you're made of iron. Never let him know if you're hurting. If you're hurting, you shouldn't be on the court. If you're on the court, you're not hurting."

This was the spartan philosophy of the spartan Aussie coach Hopman, a taskmaster to make Vince Lombardi appear almost casual. Or, better, compare them as equals, the punishing Lombardi and the callous Hopman. Each, on occasion, treated the men over whom he had absolute power as pawns, won their hatred in equal portions with their respect. Each was virtually deified and each, on occasion, was loathed. And each, assuredly, produced winners by the bushel, Hopman with any number of Davis

Cup triumphs and Lombardi with any number of National Football League championships.

"They were more afraid of Hopman than anyone across the net," writes Arthur Ashe in his book with Frank Deford, *Portrait in Motion*, of the great Aussies in Hopman's stable: Sedgman and McGregor, Anderson and Cooper, Rosewall and Hoad, Laver and Emerson, Newcombe and Roche. "The younger Aussies, the ones who never had the benefit of Hopman, are different. They don't have the same spirit and outlook. The money has changed a lot of things. Hopman probably couldn't turn things his way anymore. He treated newcomers to the squad with contempt. Here was some hotshot kid, junior champion, the comer, and Hopman made him into an errand boy, an orange squeezer." Laver came through this meat-grinder and emerged at the very top, a millionaire. "There is no one who can blow any hotter than Rocket," Ashe noted. "In 1968, in the finals of the Pacific Southwest, Rosewall beat him 7–5 in the first set, and then didn't win another game—love and love, a double bagel. When Laver goes on one of those tears, it's just ridiculous. He starts hitting the lines, and then he starts hitting the lines harder—and harder and harder. No one can stop him."

Rod Laver's left arm, and the rest of him, arrived on the earth in Rockhampton, a city of some 30,000 in the cattle country of Queensland in Australia, on August 9, 1938, in an area where almost everyone played tennis for recreation. His father, Roy Laver, owned a cattle ranch and had a passion for tennis and, with it, the conviction that his oldest son Trevor had a champion's potential. Roy played the game by the hour with his oldest boy and with his second son, Bob, but not so much with his youngest lad Rod who seemed too small and, besides, was six years younger than Trevor and four younger than Bob, and of course with youngsters a spread of that many years is hugely significant.

At any rate, a family friend named Charlie Hollis, a tennis coach in Rockhampton, disagreed with Roy's assessment and by the time Rod was ten and had been wielding a racquet for nearly seven years, it was he on whom Hollis squinted most fondly.

"Trevor and Bob are like you, Roy," Charlie Hollis pronounced one evening at the Laver home. "They're too quick-tempered, they blow up too fast. Rodney has the easy-going manner of his Mum. If we can develop a tough instinct for winning in that lad, then it'll be the perfect blend."

Rod began climbing out of bed at 5 A.M. to travel to Charlie's club for lessons. They'd play for two hours before school, return for more tennis in the late afternoons and evenings. Rod spent whatever other spare time he could find in Charlie's shop, stringing racquets, squeezing a metal spring and tennis balls to cover that left wrist and forearm with muscles. Hollis taught him proper grips, footwork, tactics, strategy, and drilled into him the importance of a winning attitude. "Your job is to go onto the court and win as quickly as possible, Rodney," Charlie stressed. "If you can beat your man 6–0 6–0, *do it!* If you let up, he can come back at you."

When eager Charlie's pupil was twelve, the coach entered his name in Queensland's junior championships in the sixteen-and-under division, a move strongly opposed by Roy Laver who figured his son could incur a demoralizing setback at an impressionable age. But Charlie persevered, and Roy personally drove young Rodney a couple of hundred miles over the rutted dusty roads of the outback to the tournament. Little Rodney was by no means outclassed; he lost the final to brother Bob by the narrowest of margins. At thirteen he won the under-fourteen state championship of Queensland at the capital, Brisbane, his first experience on grass. Until then, he'd played mostly on the court at home built by his father Roy who leveled thousands of tiny ant hills, packed them hard and rolled them smooth to produce what the future champion once recalled as being "the best clay surface in the world."

When Rod was fourteen his father and Hollis took him to a coaching clinic in Brisbane, 500 miles from the ranch, where the legendary Hopman was in charge. "Hop," said Charlie, "I have this lad from Rockhampton. He's got it, Hop; he's going to be a champion."

Hopman was scarcely prepared by this introduction for the skinny bow-legged youngster staring stolidly and shyly at the ground, shifting from one foot to the other.

"So this is the Rockhampton Rocket, is it?" said Hopman. "Okay, Rocket, let's see you serve a couple."

So the youngster served and rallied with another of Hopman's large class of students, and the Aussie coach soon knew he had a candidate for stardom. Laver learned a good deal during the clinic, returned to his sessions with Hollis in Rockhampton until he was eighteen. Hollis drove him hard. "I would end a session with every muscle aching but the pain would be gone by the next day and Charlie would start all over again," he recalled once. "He always told me that if I wanted to be a great player I would have to hit over the ball."

At that stage, before he developed his remarkable top-spin backhand, Laver followed the pattern of most left-handers of undercutting backhand shots, a method that seems almost second-nature to people born with a predominant left hand, a sort of physiological characteristic. So Charlie chanted endlessly, "Get under the ball and hit over it—under and over, under and over."

Assessing Laver's game in later years, the wily Julius Heldman lauded that unusual shot and its "incredible speed and accuracy."

"His timing, eye and wrist action are nothing short of miraculous," Heldman applauded. "On either side, forehand and backhand, he takes a full roundhouse-loop crack at the ball, which goes back so hard it can knock the racquet out of (an opponent's) hand. I saw Rod play Rafe Osuna in the semi-finals at Forest Hills in 1962. It was murder. In the last game, Rafe bravely served and ran for the net. Rod cracked a backhand back full speed, free swing—so hard that Rafe's racquet wavered in his hand. Not so amazing, perhaps, but the same scene was repeated four points in a row. Rod literally knocked Osuna down with four successive returns of serve, and Osuna was one of the quickest and best racquet handlers who ever played."

The launching of the Rocket began on a broad scale in 1956 when he was eighteen. An Australian millionaire provided $12,000 for him to tour for five months with another promising youngster, Bob Mark, under Hopman's steely gaze. Laver was ousted in the first round at the French Championships and at Wimbledon, though he and Mark did well enough in their junior matches. En route home, Rod won the Canadian and then the American junior championships, and showed enough promise during the tour to be listed as the sixth player on the Australian Davis Cup team in 1957. He played no matches but gained experience, and of course prospered under Hopman's endless drills, bike riding, road running, weight lifting, and hammering tennis balls.

He was in the wings in this fashion again in 1958, then made the team a year later for the challenge of the defending American champions at Forest Hills. He lost both singles matches—to Barry Mackay and to the Peruvian transplant Alex Olmedo. Meanwhile he'd returned twice to Wimbledon and to Forest Hills, scuttled 6–1, 6–1, 6–4 by the Czech left-hander Jaroslav Drobny on the English grass and doing somewhat better on the American turf, losing 8–6, 9–7, 6–4 to the powerful Dick Savitt in 1958.

It was obvious he'd be around for awhile by the time he reached Forest Hills in September 1959 for the U.S. nationals. There, in numerous long matches, he struggled to the finals in singles and men's doubles, playing nearly 800 games in five days. In the singles semis he engaged Mackay again in an exhausting match, finally emerging by 11–13, 11–9, 10–8, 7–9, and 6–3. In that concluding set he trailed by 3–1 and still somehow managed to walk erectly, head high, in the accepted Australian manner after eighty-two games. Then, remarkably, he ran off five straight games.

But that marathon took its toll, and Laver had little to throw at Alex Olmedo in the final; he went out in straight sets.

By now, Laver's was a recognized name at center court everywhere. He had shown steady improvement in his three years of touring and had made a strong impression overall. Still, the fact remained that he had won nothing, and as he returned to Australia late in 1959 there was the gnawing chance that he was a perennial bridesmaid.

The label was partially dispelled early in 1960 when he won his first major championship, the Australian, against countryman Neale Fraser. There, he climbed over the hump in a five-setter, a cliff-hanging 8–6 in the fifth. But then he lost in the finals at both Wimbledon and Forest Hills to that same deft left-hander Fraser, highly significant tournaments at which to be left at the altar.

There was a certain improvement in 1961—losses to Roy Emerson, sure enough, in both the Australian and American championships in the final round, but a smashing win over Chuck McKinley in the most prestigious tournament of all, the grass patch at Wimbledon.

The appearance of Laver and Emerson on center court at Forest Hills that September was a tribute to the eye and the perseverance of Hopman, for Emerson owned a background as unsophisticated as Laver's. Emmo was brought up on a cattle ranch near a town called Black Butt, and he developed his wrist power by milking cows, thousands of cows. Arthur Ashe once said there were two absolutes about Emerson: "One, he is the fittest player who ever lived. Two, he is the most popular." He could play all day and all night—and he literally did, although it wasn't tennis he played at night. Outgoing and raucous, another of the legion of Aussie beer drinkers, he hated to leave a party, and was usually the last man to do so. Still, come daylight, he could tear around a tennis court as though he'd had fourteen hours of sleep, and he and the comparative stoic Laver engaged in some marvellous duels on the courts of the world. Emmo won the Australian six times, the French twice, Wimbledon twice and injuries cost him a third and possibly a fourth at the shrine. But, again, in the Australian fashion, he never allowed an injury to serve as a reason for a defeat.

And Emerson always seemed to be the man across the net in the final round as Laver endeavored to reach his announced goal in 1962: the Grand Slam. Three times they met in the ultimate round of the four big tournaments, and three times Laver was able to come away with the national crown (indeed, they even met in the final of the Italian Championships in Rome, though Italy is not Slam country). Laver won in four sets on the White City courts of Sydney in the Australian in January, then won in five sets over Emmo in the French in Paris after a semifinal against Neale Fraser that nearly undid him; he trailed 4–5 in the fifth with Fraser serving but then prevailed and moved across the Channel to England, still unblemished.

For once, Emerson was a spectator when Laver stepped onto the courts for a final-round match—this time in late June at Wimbledon when an unknown meteor named Marty Mulligan, yet another Aussie, was the other finalist. Mulligan had a great year in 1962, unknown before and largely unheard of since. In the quarterfinals in Paris he'd had Laver at match point and then, at Wimbledon, he'd sprinted through his half of the draw to reach center court in the final. There was no repetition of the Paris debacle this time; Laver quelled this upstart in straight sets.

Now he needed to win at Forest Hills to join Donald Budge as the only player ever to win the Slam. To get him away from the endless interviews and mounting pressure of his impending feat, Budge himself stepped forward gallantly to invite Laver to play a relaxed match in a Catskill mountains resort but, really, the day only added to the pressure, bringing Laver face to face in a tennis setting with the man who'd done the deed.

Yet he whistled through the early rounds in spite of the attention that followed him everywhere, and waiting for him across the net as the final moment dawned was, of course, the slick-haired, swift-moving, determined and endlessly competitive Emmo. However, this was not the time for Laver to allow his friend to direct a detour, as he had often done; no, this time the scrawny left-hander was not to be denied. He even began uncharacteristically swiftly, racing off to a two-set lead in spite of anything Emmo could throw up against him: tough serves, crisp volleys, and unbounded enthusiasm and guts. Emerson reversed the tide in the third set, but only momentarily, and when Laver won the fourth he had completed the Grand Slam and joined the masters. He cemented his position with two singles victories in Australia's Davis Cup achievement and, looking around, he realized that all that remained now were the professionals. Not sure he could beat 'em, he joined 'em—on January 4, 1963, a three-year contract guaranteeing him $100,000 and making the transition utterly painless.

The painlessness lasted exactly two days. On January 5 at Sydney's White City, Laver went in against Lew Hoad, the Australian giant of the mid-1950s who'd missed the Grand Slam by the margin of the U.S. nationals in 1956 after he'd swept the first three legs. Pancho Gonzales once said that if there were a Universe David Cup Hoad was the man he'd pick to represent Earth to play one match the planet had to win. He was, in Arthur Ashe's phrase, "colorful and charismic," and if back trouble hadn't done him in he might well have hastened the tennis boom by a decade. Anyway, Hoad did a thorough job on Laver in the latter's professional debut, dropping the first set at 8–6 and then running out the match in straight sets.

One day later, it was Ken Rosewall's turn, and little Muscles did an even more savage job, yielding only three games in each of the three sets. "Muscles hits every backhand the same—perfect," Ashe wrote once. "So much attention is paid his backhand that almost nobody ever gets around to mentioning his volley, which is positively the best in the world."

As these three gilded Aussies moved into their overseas tour, Laver seldom found peace, sweet peace. Hoad added three more victories over him and Rosewall two before he finally won a match, shading Rosewall. This was the pattern for three months, the more experienced pair of pros making mincemeat of Laver's world-class game. Sometimes he'd go a week without beating either of them; overall, he averaged about one win every five matches. In the world's top pro tournament at England's Wembley in September he was knocked out early by the American Butch Buchholz. The pros were untrammeled by his volleys, and ripped his second serve to shreds. When they toured the U.S. Laver found conditions far removed from the first-class life he'd known as an amateur. Often they played eight or ten matches in eight or ten towns on consecutive nights, driving their cars hundreds of miles across the countryside by day, tottering red-eyed onto all manner of courts by night.

This was the life Laver knew—and the others, too—for five years, and by then he and Rosewall were the undisputed top professionals. During these years, a campaign for open tennis slowly swelled and it reached its apex in August of 1967 when Wimbledon opened its gates to a professional tournament for the first time and, more, announced that beginning in 1968 the hallowed All-England Championship, the one known everywhere simply as Wimbledon, would not be confined to amateurs only; it would truly be a test for *all* the world's top players.

That decision routed the forces who favored retention of the old hypocrisy, the division between pros and "shamateurs." Wimbledon's prestige was too powerful to be shunned by the bigots, though the caterwauling was fierce. Britain was threatened with nothing short of ostracism by the International Lawn Tennis Federation but, in the end, the ILTF reluctantly embraced the principle of open tennis in an historic decision on March 30, 1968.

Surprisingly, the amateurs did much better against the pros than had been anticipated. Arthur Ashe, Dennis Ralston, Mark Cox, and others scored victories that could only be called upsets, and these surprises were attributable in most cases to the fact the amateurs felt they had nothing to lose while the pros were taut and tense in trying to demonstrate their superior skills.

Laver, though, prevailed in that first Open Wimbledon, knocking off Ashe in the semifinal and countryman Tony Roche in the final. "The professionals will not be under such great pressure in the opens that follow," Laver philosophized. "Now it will be the amateurs who have to live up to their records. They have got to prove they can keep on doing it."

With open tennis everywhere, Laver undertook in 1969 to become the first player to sweep the Grand Slam boards, amateur *and* pro, but his ambition almost died aborning. In January that year he played the most gruelling match of his career, before or since, in the semifinals of the Australian Open in the 105-degree heat of Brisbane, even longer and more arduous than his eighty-seven games against Barry MacKay at Wimbledon ten years earlier.

In this one he faced the hulking muffin-faced left-hander Tony Roche, another product of the Australian outback, a marvellous player from a tiny town called Tarcutta who, like Lew Hoad, was prevented from attaining his place in the sun by injury.

But there was nothing wrong with him on that scorching January afternoon in 1969 when play started at noon and was not completed until four hours later. As a young player Laver had often stuffed wet cabbage leaves into a brimmed white hat to ward off the sun, and this day he could well have done with a head or two of the stuff. As it was, he soaked three sunhats through the ordeal, gulped glucose and salt tablets, and both players, in changing ends, draped themselves in towels lifted from iceboxes at courtside.

Laver won the first two sets and appeared in no great difficulty, though Roche had forced him to 7–5 and a marathon 22–20. Then Roche showed superior conditioning in the third set, winning 11–9, and Laver trudged gratefully to a shower and clothes change at the intermission. Roche could hardly wait to get at him in the fourth set, and ran off five straight games as though the match were just beginning. In fact, they'd now played seventy-nine games in their overheated oven.

Laver knew the fourth set was gone, trailing 0–5, but he wanted badly to win his service and get to 1–5. That way, with Roche closing out the set on his serve, Laver would lead off the decisive set as the server. He won his serve, and Roche his for 6–1. "It's a psychological help to go into the lead every time you win your serve in a close match," Laver wrote later. "That's why I tried so hard for a seemingly meaningless game when I was down 0–5. I figured one break of serve would decide the match, the condition we were in. Tony was stronger, but he'd never been in a fifth set with me and, serving second, he'd have just a little more pressure on him."

He kept getting his first serve in, and volleying well, and the deciding set went along as he'd hoped it might. One–love for Laver, one–all, 2–1, 2–2, 3–2, 3–3, 4–3. Each time Roche went to the service line he found himself trailing by a game, and that built the pressure.

"It was his turn to serve and I screwed my mind into working for every point as though it were the last," Laver penned later in his book, written with Bud Collins and called *The Education of a Tennis Player.* "If you do that when you come down the stretch in a tight match you'll be surprised how often a superhuman effort will come out of you."

And so it was a vital game. They split the first two points, then Roche missed a volley, then Laver returned Roche's serve crosscourt and Roche looked relieved that

133

the return had gone out, making it 30–30. But, wait, there was no linesman's call. Could the ball have been in? Roche turned to the linesman and, to his dismay, the linesman was holding out his hands, palms down, meaning the ball was *good*. Roche was dumbfounded. Instead of being even at 30–30, he now trailed 15–40, a terrifying difference. Roche couldn't believe it. He was furious. When he went to serve again, the call was still nagging. And with two points to spare Laver put everything he had into a topspin backhand down the line—*everything*. Roche anticipated the shot—it was a Laver favorite—but, even so, it was loaded with so much spin and pace, Laver had hit it so viciously that Roche couldn't handle it. Laver's game. Laver's serve. Laver's lead, 5–3. It was all so unfair, Roche felt, that he had nothing left to counter with. Laver ran out his service, won the set and the match, and fell into the shower after ninety sun-scorched games. And what it all proved, of course, was Laver's contention that no one—*no* one—can ever afford to dwell on the injustice of an official's call.

Though Laver was now thirty years old—he'd turn thirty-one before getting to Forest Hills for the fourth leg of his Slam goal—he came off this grind against Roche in good shape for the final. He encountered only modest resistance from Spain's Andres Gimeno in it and won in straight sets.

He always found the slow clay of Roland Garros difficult whenever he engaged in the French Championships, but this time Paris was a pleasure. In his seven matches there, only the lithe and bounding Tom Okker of the Netherlands was able to win even a set, and the final against the redoubtable Rosewall found Laver at the absolute peak of his game, his drives off both sides going so deep that Muscles was rarely able to fight his way to the net for his devastating volleys.

And so it was on to Wimbledon where Laver sought his fourth championship on that royal grass and where, this time, he found endless obstacles. As early as the fourth round, engaging America's Stan Smith, he was in deep trouble after running off the first two sets. The elongated Smith with his enormous reach got his serve-and-volley game together then, and pulled even in sets, and constantly attacked Laver's serves though just failing to break through in the fifth.

Laver got a solitary service break to lead 5–3, but he was down 0–40 serving the ninth game and, of course, in jeopardy. A break here, he said later, "would have put wings" on Smith's game and perhaps have spelled the difference. But as he had done so many times in this situation Laver came up with the quality that set him apart. He won five straight points to run out the match.

Next it was Arthur Ashe, a streak player at the top of a streak, nearly blowing Laver off the court in the first set. Laver stemmed the assault in the second set, barely pulled out the third at 9–7, then sent Ashe reeling off into the strawberry patches with a love-set mop-up in the fourth.

The final obstacle was John Newcombe, the prowling, crashing mustachioed Aussie who'd won at Wimbledon in 1967 (and would win again in 1970 and 1971). After two sets they were even, and Newk pulled ahead in the third, then romped to a 4–1 lead in the fourth. Here again the match may have hung on a single shot. Newk had Laver in the predicament where, had he knocked a backhand down the line, he'd have gone on top by 5–1. But he didn't. He tried a crosscourt shot that Laver volleyed for a winner, and that steadied Laver, got him rolling, set him on his way to a 6–4 win in that set and another by the same count in the fifth of a classic match.

Now he had four Wimbledon championships, a unique feat, and was one tournament removed from his second Slam, another unique feat. What was no unique feat was that Laver got what he needed when he needed it. He brushed past troublesome spots represented by his old friend Roy Emerson and two Americans, Ashe and Denny Ralston, and then caught Tony Roche in a difficult bind. Rain fell on the morning of the final and the grass courts Forest Hills knew in that era were soft. Roche had a pulled leg muscle so sufficiently severe that he feared to wear spikes on the slow turf. Thus it was not the Roche of the 105-degree heat in Brisbane that Laver handled easily this day in New York.

Now the Rocket had reached the pinnacle. Endorsements flowed like wine and he continued to win on the courts, as he was doing, indeed, even a decade later on occasion. In that year of 1969 he became the first player to win more than $100,000 in a twelve-month period, and not long afterwards he became the first to win more than a million dollars, a scrawny bow-legged little virtuoso who climbed out from under cabbage leaves to mingle with kings.

ARTHUR ASHE

[1943–   ]

ARTHUR ASHE won two tennis tournaments seven years apart that were enough to elevate his place in the firmament from being remarkable because he was black to remarkable because he was good. Not merely good, but outstanding. And the two, of course, were *the* two—Forest Hills in 1968 and Wimbledon in 1975. What other two are there?

Oh, Ashe won all sorts of tournaments in between. He won the Australian Open in 1970, the Stockholm Open in 1972, and he won in places like Montreal and Rome, Rotterdam and Louisville, Bologna and Barcelona. Ashe won any number of Davis Cup matches and in 1972 he became the first American to win more than $100,000 in prize money. Still, there was a link missing somewhere in his persona as a tennis player even as late as 1974, something lacking in his makeup that prevented him from gaining more than grudging recognition. He was too placid, too indifferent to whether he won or lost. There was no emotion, no ability, or perhaps desire, to come up off the floor. If he won, he won; if he lost, he lost.

Billie Jean King, the fiercely competitive leader of the women's revolution on the courts and in the committee rooms, summed it up once: "Arthur Ashe has great natu-

Arthur Ashe

ral talent but he'll never win an important title unless he becomes a competitor. Arthur just doesn't care enough." She said that at Hilton Head in South Carolina in October 1973, five years after Ashe had won at Forest Hills and she wasn't being catty. That's simply how people felt about Arthur Ashe. The U.S. crown in 1968 seemed to have slipped their minds.

Where he turned it all around was at Wimbledon in 1975. And the significance was not just that he won there; it was also that he beat Jimmy Connors, who was at the top of his game and the bottom of his manners in that period, graceless and boorish. Beat him as the rank underdog at odds of 2 to 11 in the British bookmakers' salons. Beat him soundly and solidly, 6–1, 6–1, 5–7, and 6–4. Beat him by shutting him off when it appeared he might be coming back. Beat him by, of all things, being competitive.

The charge against Ashe was essentially that he had no killer's instinct, that when he got an opponent down he refused to kick him in the accepted mode of modern pro sports. Consequently, a lot of times he'd rush into quick and devastating leads and then lose his edge and fail in matches he appeared to have well in hand. It wasn't that he gave up if an opponent came back at him; no, it was just that he seemed to lose his concentration, or his interest, or both, come back into contention occasionally and then, more often than not, fade off into the sunset.

Typical of this sort of thing was Ashe's 1968 semifinal match with Rod Laver at Wimbledon, the very year, ironically enough, that he returned to America to win Forest Hills a few months later. At Wimbledon, though, his exit seemed entirely Ashian.

This was the first of the open tournaments in high places, the year Wimbledon thumbed its aristocratic nose at the amateur panjandrums who had persistently refused to accept the pros in the classic tournaments. Ashe was still technically an amateur; indeed, he was technically a soldier, a lieutenant in the U.S. Army playing tennis coast-to-coast at home, in England, and in Australia. Wimbledon was part of that curious khaki odyssey. He'd staggered to the semis by surviving five-setters with the obscure South African Terry Ryan and the equally unheralded Briton Graham Stillwell.

When he went in against Laver, though, he played the first set, in the Australian master's words, "as well as a man can play, far above anything I had imagined for him." Lashed 6–2, Laver's thoughts were that if Ashe kept up the pace it was curtains for him. "When Arthur is playing that well, there's not much to do about it except hope that he cools," Laver wrote later. "Arthur's history tells you he's streaky and won't keep it up forever." He didn't this day in 1968, either. He came back tough in the third set after Laver caught up to him in the second, but then he faded off in his own special way and was whipped, 2–6, 6–2, 9–7, 6–0.

A year later when Laver was on his way to his second Grand Slam, Ashe once again was his semifinal opponent at Wimbledon. On reflection Laver had similar observations that expressed the general feeling about Ashe in spite of his having won Forest Hills the previous September. This time Arthur's serve was humming. "It's a tremendous serve," Later noted, almost in passing, "but often that's all there is to Arthur. He's bang-bang, thrash-thrash, and the points come in clusters. Unhappily for him, there are too many stretches of clunk-clunk." Laver won the match by 8–6, 6–3, and 14–12 and remarked as he went to the locker room that Ashe should have won the first and third sets. Then he embellished the observation: "When I say he should have won those sets, I mean the opportunity was there for a guy who could fasten his mind on the right approach and lock out everything else. Arthur just doesn't do that—he admits it himself—and until he can he won't be a great player."

As Laver said—"he admits it himself"—Ashe's mind wanders, but approaching the mid-1970s Ashe put a different interpretation on the reasons for it. "We've never had this situation in tennis before where players at the top have been challenged year after year," he records in a diary called *Arthur Ashe: Portrait in Motion* which he put together with the help of Frank Deford as an account of life on the circuit from Wimbledon 1973 to Wimbledon 1974. "You're on the line, week after week." He draws an analogy between the tennis pro's predicament and the pro golfer's, noting that the latter can have an off day in a tournament and still come back and win; a 74 doesn't necessarily knock him out of contention. On the pro tennis player's off day, though—the day on which he plays the equivalent of a round of 74—he can be knocked out.

And there's no question that Ashe's heart belongs to the game as he records the lilt of a high moment: "When I'm playing well I can be almost euphoric out on the court. I just feel terrific. The thing is, at any time, whoever is across the net, you are never really playing an opponent. You are playing yourself, your own highest standards, and when you reach your limits there is real joy. It does not take a whole tournament, even a whole match, to get that feeling. If you are playing your best, you can attain it with just one shot. I remember one time when Tom (Gorman) drove me into the corner, and I returned with a winner, a chip backhand cross-court deep. Perfect. I can still see myself: moving over, planting the left foot just so, reaching back with the racquet, bringing it across, following through high and away. Perfect. Unreal so perfect. The ball sails right where it is supposed to go. Suddenly, the essence of everything you have worked a lifetime for is distilled into one shot."

This was the man who faced Connors in Wimbledon's center court in 1975 carrying the bookmakers' coldly impartial disregard as an 11–2 underdog. In retrospect it's difficult to imagine that anyone—anyone—could have felt differently about the outcome, with the exception of Ashe himself, envisioning a day filled with the kind of shot he described making against Gorman. Certainly none of his peers was anticipating an upset against a Connors who had not dropped even a set in rushing through to the final. Certainly Billie Jean King and Rod Laver, judging by their assessment of the enigmatic Arthur Ashe, were anticipating none.

Ashe went into this match with excessive preparation. He had the full-hearted cooperation of the American Davis Cup team captain Donald Dell if for no other reason than that he was a team member and Connors was, by choice, not. Dell wanted the services of the two-fisted player with the cannonading pace but, for one reason and another, Connors declined to join the team. So Dell went to pains during Wimbledon to accumulate the opinions of various knowledgeable players on ways to beat

Connors. These included Charlie Pasarell, Fred McNair, Marty Riessen, and Dennis Ralston, who alone contributed four pages of notes from previous Connors' matches. Dell then distilled this information, and transferred five essential points to a slip of paper that Ashe wore under a sweatband on his left wrist during his match. As it turned out, Ashe had committed these five essentials so thoroughly to memory that he did not refer to the notes at all as he engaged Connors.

Ashe had good reason to bring all of his concentration to bear, apart from any tennis player's understandable desire to win at Wimbledon. Not long before the tournament began, he was named by Connors in a $3 million libel and slander suit for his criticism of Connors' refusal to play Davis Cup. More, Connors had another multimillion dollar suit against the Association of Tennis Professionals—of which Ashe was president, no less.

Ashe's competitive approach to the match was to warm up strenuously until five minutes before he was due on the court, then get a vigorous massage. He and Dell were aware that he is a slow starter, that Connors is a tiger on the court from the opening toss.

One of the five points in the game plan took into account an acknowledged Connors' forte, his vicious return of serve, a bullet from either side. Accordingly, Ashe planned to keep his serves wide, aiming for the tapes on both forehand and backhand so that Connors would have to stretch to reach them, and although Connors' speed of foot and movement are strong parts of his game, Ashe is a man who can deliver cannonballs from the service line. By keeping them wide, then, he hoped to reduce Connors' effectiveness in this department.

But perhaps the most effective tactic in Ashe's bag, as it turned out, was his and Dell's then revolutionary theory that the best way to counter Connors' enormous pace was to feed him soft stuff and force him to provide his own velocity rather than turn the speed of his opponent's shots to his own advantage. So the plan was to employ drop shots and lobs, especially short low dinks to the somewhat restricted reach of Connors on his two-fisted backhand. "It may have looked suicidal at first," Ashe said afterwards, "but I gave it a lot of thought and talked to lots of people about how to play him."

Yet it's one thing to plan strategy and quite another to bring off the shots that turn theory into action. On this particular day, Ashe had the shots. He lost the first game of the match and then, to the astonishment of a world-wide television audience, won nine in a row. He ran out the first set at 6–1 in 20 minutes and repeated the medicine in the second set, this time in 25 minutes. One thing about Connors, he never stopped battling, scrambling, hammering away. At one point a voice in the throng called, "Come *on*, Connors!" And Connors shouted back, "I'm *tryin'*, for chrissake!"

And in the third set the anxious moments for the thousands backing the underdog—sentimentally, if not with their money—began to rise. Connors *was* coming back. Ashe *was* reverting to form. He *was* beginning to fade at the precise moment when he appeared to have everything well in hand. It *was* turning into a typical Ashe performance.

Connors, scrambling doggedly, broke Ashe to take a 4–2 lead in the third set, then fought off two break points to win the next game and go ahead 5–2. Ashe got it even at 5–5 but then Connors again averted an Ashe game by beating off two breakers, and holding himself for a 7–5 win. Launched at last, he broke into a 3–0 lead in the fourth set.

Here was the crucible for Ashe; here was the moment at which he'd dozed off so many times before. Changing sides on the odd game, he sat on a wooden chair beside the umpire's chair, immobile, eyes closed. Then he roused himself, went to the service line and ran out a quick game. Next, he broke Connors, trailing 30–40 and dropping a chip for deuce, smashing an overhead to get the advantage, rifling a forehand down the line to pull it out. At 4–4 he drifted a backhand to the corner that Connors ignored, thinking it was floating out. He chipped another for another point, then drilled a backhand down the line. Leading 15–40 he broke Connors by feeding him a short soft drop shot that Connors volleyed into the net. Now Ashe was serving for the match. A calm controlled stoic, he rammed his big serve into the corners and won as unconcernedly as if he were banging a ball against a fence at sunrise. He was as unemotional in interviews afterwards. He noted that Connors sent the heavy majority of his errors into the net. "He hardly ever put the ball beyond the baseline on his errors," Ashe rubbed it in. "That's a sign of choking." It was apparent that Arthur Ashe had heard the story one too many times that he was streaky, that there were too many stretches of clunk-clunk, that he couldn't fasten his mind to a project.

Arthur Robert Ashe, Jr., was born in a middle-class black neighborhood in Richmond, Virginia, on July 10,

1943, son of a recreation-department policeman whose wife died when Arthur was six. It is hardly necessary to relate that at that time in that place, all of Arthur Ashe's playmates were black, or to dwell on the point that he was not allowed to play in any of the parks where white kids romped. That's the way it was in the land of the free in the 1940s and the 1950s when Arthur Ashe was growing up.

His father, Arthur, Sr., was left with two sons when his wife died, the other just twenty-one months old. He got a housekeeper, Olis Berry, to help him look after his house and his boys and, to accommodate this additional expense he scrubbed people's floors and cut their grass when he wasn't being a recreation-department policeman. "I prayed every night I would raise them right," he said once of his sons. "They were good boys, they never fought. I taught Arthur to be patient. I told him things don't change in a day." In due course, Arthur, Sr., was married again and added two children to the family. In 1953 Florence was born and, a year later, Robert.

Black kids don't get into tennis much. Not many of them have families who can afford racquets and balls and, of course, club memberships are out of the question as well as, in most areas, out of bounds. But there were courts in one of the recreation parks where Arthur, Sr., worked, Brook Field, and young Arthur, tall and lean early in his adolescence, had an affinity for the game. This affinity was spotted by Ronald Charity, a Richmond playground director, who mentioned it to Dr. R. W. Johnson, a black physician in Lynchburg, Virginia, who had the money and the disposition to help young black tennis players, rare as they were. One of those he'd helped was a young Harlem stringbean named Althea Gibson, who played paddleball on the sidewalks of New York and climbed, under Johnson's benign eye, to the center court at Wimbledon and the one at Forest Hills where she won twice each in the final round.

Johnson took Arthur Ashe to the same lawn court at his home in Lynchburg on which he'd taught Althea Gibson. He was sufficiently pleased by Ashe's progress that when the boy was fourteen he began to enter his name in junior tournaments. A year later Arthur gained the semifinals of the sixteen-and-under division, and when he was seventeen and eighteen he won the national junior indoor championship. By the time he'd graduated from high school at eighteen, young Ashe was ranked twenty-eighth in the nation, and that was good enough for the University of California at Los Angeles. The Uclans offered him an athletic scholarship, providing books, board, and tuition in exchange for his tennis talents and 250 hours worth of his working time in the campus dining room. Not entirely unexpectedly, Arthur accepted the offer.

On the hard courts of the soft climate he met the redoubtable Richard Pancho Gonzales, a member of a minority group himself, who lived near the UCLA campus and occasionally dropped by to help the athletic director and tennis coach, J. D. Morgan. Gonzales spent many an hour making it painfully clear to Ashe that he had an enormous amount to learn about tennis—and helping him close the gap. "I felt comfortable around him," Ashe said once. "His skin was nearly the color of mine. He had a special tennis mind; he could look at you hit the ball once and diagnose all your mistakes."

Within two years Ashe had climbed from twenty-eighth to sixth in the national rankings. He was third in 1964, and second in the ensuing three years. In 1968 when he won at Forest Hills he was accorded the No. 1 position. By then, he had become a veteran Davis Cupper. Back in that UCLA period of 1963 he made his first appearance for his country and by 1970 he'd won twenty-four out of twenty-seven singles matches. In 1965 at Christmas he went to Australia with the American team, and won three out of four state championships there, beating Roy Emerson, John Newcombe, and Fred Stolle at Melbourne, Brisbane, and Adelaide. Since he was then twenty-two years old, Pancho Gonzales was to say of him: "He is the most promising player in the world today."

Coming back from Australia just past New Year's 1966, Ashe went immediately into the Army. Since he'd been a UCLA major in business administration, he was assigned to the data processing office of the military academy at West Point as a lieutenant and allowed to keep his tennis racquet out of its press, playing Davis Cup and in 1967 travelling to Winnipeg, Manitoba, for the Pan Am games in that Canadian city, and then moving on to Australia for the championships there.

The year 1968 was his last as an amateur—and as a soldier. He played in New York, Philadelphia, and Sacramento before leaping across the Atlantic for that first confrontation with Laver at Wimbledon in which he ripped the Aussie to shreds in the first set and then began to think of things like forced marches or k.p. duty or whatever for the rest of the match. He came home to win the U.S. Amateur at Brookline, Massachusetts, the first American to win that one in thirteen years, and by the time he got to Forest Hills he was riding a twenty-match winning streak.

It was a curious Forest Hills that year. All the newly emancipated professionals were allowed on the sacred turf—led by the fantastic foursome from Australia: Laver, Newcombe, Roche, and Rosewall. The ubiquitous oddsmakers of London were booking the event, and had 30 to 1 against an amateur winning. But the big guns kept silencing one another, or being knocked off by lightly regarded opponents. For instance, Cliff Drysdale eliminated Laver, and Gonzales, now forty, tripped up Roche. Ashe kayoed Emerson in straight sets, and Rosewall was put away by Tom Okker. Newcombe went out, too, so that when the final round came along, who should be stepping into the horseshoe center court but Arthur Ashe and the tiny speedball from Holland, Okker.

They had a great match for the 14,000 at the West Side Tennis Club, all of whom were set on edge by the chilling first set in which Ashe finally prevailed at 14–12. Okker, a catlike young man, handsome and curly-haired and wondrously fluid of motion, got even at 7–5, then dropped back before the intermission at 6–3. He came out from the shower and change of raiment swinging from both sides and evened the match 6–3. Was this another Ashe flip-out? No, not this time. Arthur got that big serve singing and won his first major championship with a 6–3 fifth-set. The old American champion Jack Kramer, calling the shots for television, was to observe after Ashe had delivered his final cannonball: "This week, at least, Arthur Ashe has proven himself to be the best player in the world. His improvement astonishes me."

But in the years ahead after Ashe turned professional upon his release from the army in February 1969, the only thing that really astonished people was the lackadaisical nature of his ways on the court. Until 1975 and Jimmy Connors, that is.

ILIE NASTASE

[1946–   ]

THE RIDDLE OF ILIE NASTASE has baffled behavioral scien-
tists from Argentina to Zanzibar, not just as the crow flies
but also as the alphabet flows, a man who stirs up his
unique witch's brew in any of the globe's corners large
enough to attract a tennis mercenary.

The pest of Bucharest, the Rumanian rogue, Ilie
emerged in the first half of the decade of the 1970s as a
conundrum to cloud men's minds (and women's too).
Amateur and professional psychologists have spent hours
probing the dilemma of this marvellously gifted player
with the unpredictable court deportment, summed up
once by the television commentator and skilled player
Julie Heldman. "Ilie has the legs and the temperament of
a race horse," said she, and that says an awful lot about
Nasty.

Nastase has been called a surly, abusive, spoiled buf-
foon. His on-court profanity and gestures when he is
upset are crude, rude, boorish, and, if a spectator happens to be a trifle squeamish, downright shocking. No
word that Nasty can lay tongue to is safe when he skids
into one of his patented tantrums, and he *shouts* them at
offending linesmen, umpires, spectators, or opponents

Ilie Nastase

with no regard whatever for the sensitivity of innocent bystanders.

For all this, though, unforgivable as it often seems, there is a curious childlike quality to Nastase that tends to take the edge off even his most outrageous behavior. It's almost as though a five-year-old had been handed this vocabulary and this slim six-foot physique. Other times, there's a mischievous cunning discernible in his mood. On these occasions he'll mock the person across the net from him, or patronize him, or be maddeningly solicitous. If his opponent misses an easy shot, Nasty is apt to offer him his racquet as a substitute. He does things that unhinge people. When he plays tall cannon-serving players like, say, Australia's John Alexander, he doesn't end rallies as quickly as he might. He likes to run them in the heat and he will prolong points to keep them running so that the advantage of their power is dissipated. He is wily, astonishingly quick, and a master of anticipation, a glowering, volatile, intimidating . . . well, *cad*. He has built up such a backlog of turbulence over the years that even when he is on his best behavior his opponents sense an uneasy truce. Nasty is a sly Vesuvius.

No one really knows what to make of him, though just about everybody has taken a run at it. Dr. Joyce Brothers, the psychologist, writer, and TV person, believes Nastase's actions are premeditated, which is not a universally held conviction by any means. "Because tennis is considered a gentleman's game," she says, "he keeps his opponents so shook up they can't concentrate. When he acts up he usually is psyching his opponent. Tennis is a game of concentration and flow, and anything you do to break your opponent's concentration will psych him out."

Former U.S. tennis star Allen Fox, a Ph.D. in psychology, says he finds Nastase personally charming but that he doesn't want ever to play him. "He hasn't been trained to control himself, he's not a mature individual generally, and it shows up in his court behavior."

Julie Anthony, a psychologist and ranking player, believes Nastase's blowups are a form of choking. "They're an emotional release which let him loosen up," she says. "He can't stand the pressure that builds up and I think he feels he'll blow it unless he releases his tension."

Bud Collins, the tennis telecaster, tends to share the view that Nastase can't handle pressure and, since pressure is usually toughest when a player is losing, Nastase's biggest blowups develop when he's trailing in big matches. Most notable was the Davis Cup final round in 1972 when the U.S. invaded Nastase's home grounds in Bucharest to shade Rumania by 3–2 in a turbulent three days in which linesmen's calls were often questionable and occasionally outrageous, where crowd involvement was intense, profane, and heated, and where, in Bud Collins's judgment, "Nasty simply blew it; he was terrified and he choked." Stan Smith was the U.S. star, winning both singles over Nastase and his partner, the veteran Ion Tiriac, and teaming with Erik van Dillen to win the doubles from Nastase and Tiriac.

Arthur Ashe says Nastase is "a walking paradox," an incredibly gifted and devoted athlete "who somehow can lose from 5–2 and 40–0; it is impossible to fathom him." But Ashe says that when Nasty makes fun of an opponent—"the most un-American thing of all"—he is not being malicious, as it may appear from the stands or even to an opponent, but only childish. "He is so vain he doesn't realize what he is doing to his opponent." Ashe says Nastase is so good that "I actually can get inspired watching him play."

Inspired was hardly the word for Ashe in Stockholm in December 1975 during the Masters Grand Prix in which the eight top performers from the year's tour struggled for a top prize of $40,000, with the pest of Bucharest at his best, mooching around the court, gesticulating, mumbling, grouching. In a match against Ashe in which he was trailing, he quick-served while a ball was loose on the court, and the umpire ruled the point be played over. Nasty protested, a fan yelled at him, he yelled back, gave the fan the routine Nastase middle-finger gesture, then got into a shouting exchange with the fan. Finally, he cooled sufficiently to go back to the service line, and then four times he faked as if to serve, each time stopping and calling to Ashe, "Are you ready, Mr. Ashe?" Finally, Ashe stomped off the court and subsequently was awarded the match after the Swedish nabobs had tut-tutted for hours.

The old guard of tennis freaks out every time Nastase drops into a town for a tournament, but there are a great many people who find Nastase fascinating, a colorful, unpredictable, temperamental beacon in an ocean of drab and passive pro athletes who take the money and run, or, worse, complain tediously about how difficult it is to be them—how long their seasons are, how endless the travel, how painful to perform in three time zones while crisscrossing the continental U.S. So few of them in the 1970s leap to the obvious alternative: Find work.

Nastase has no such side; he lets it all hang out, glowering, turbulent, volatile. Unlike Dr. Brothers, some psychologists aren't all that sure the Nastase number is premeditated. But even if it is, they ask, what's wrong with that? Now that tennis has been wrenched painstakingly from the secluded lawns of the wealthy, now that it has at long last shucked off its mink swaddling clothes and become a big game for the masses, why should it retain its foppish facade?

The point made on Nastase's behalf is that if a professional athlete can distract another professional athlete by whacking him over the head with a hockey stick, if he can throw a ball at somebody's head on any baseball diamond in the universe, if he can punch and kick and skewer an opponent on the football field, then why must pro tennis players be expected to behave like twits?

It's Nastase's insistence that what happens when he's on the court is simply a reflection of his teeming emotions. "Everybody is not the same," he said once. "Everybody's personality is his own. Arthur Ashe is Arthur Ashe and I am me. I don't try to make trouble; what happens outside comes from inside and I pay for it—fines, defaults, all those things."

No one is more dismayed or, indeed, baffled by Nastase's actions than his tall slender young wife Dominique, called Nikky, a wealthy Frenchwoman. "I married two men," she told Tony Kornheiser of the *New York Times,* after Nastase had made an enormous spectacle of himself in the U.S. nationals of 1976 in a match with Hans-Jurgen Pohmann of West Germany (the *Times'* account of the match had this lead paragraph: "Ilie Nastase disgraced Forest Hills yesterday," and then noted that the center-court scene "approached those in ancient Rome when the displeased customers called for the lions.").

In the Kornheiser interview, Nikky Nastase expanded on her notion of being married to two men: "There is the man I see at home, and that other man I see on the court. I love the two parts—the good and the bad. It is the special thing about Ilie, the, I don't know how you say in English. You either love him or hate him. You see, there is no middle with Ilie. I hear them bait him. I hear the crowd call him, 'Communist pig.' I hear it when they say, 'Go back to Rumania.' He cannot be cool. He has no answer. I sit here and watch until I cannot sit anymore. I get sick in my stomach sometime, and I have to leave. I can have ulcer, I think.

"I think Ilie was really crazy, really near to cry, when he play Pohmann. It was the crowd, I think. All I think is they want him to get mad on the court. Like, they pay the money and they come to see a crazy thing on the court. It was the lions and the Christians. I was waiting for them to put the thumbs down, to call for him to be killed. I don't know why he act like that. Sometimes something happens. He goes mad, I guess. I think there are times when he does not know what he is doing, when he does not know where he is. All he really wants is the crowd to enjoy him. But he cannot control himself. Sometimes I am embarrassed by it. Because the crowd does not understand him. Because he seems so mad out there. He is like a child, I guess. He just cannot keep it inside him."

No one knows, really, what to do about Nastase—or, at least, no one had come up with a solution by the time the 1977 season rolled around. Herbert Warren Wind, the gentleman from The New Yorker, grew quite haughty in the manner in which gentlemen from The New Yorker get, in suggesting that he ought to be suspended. "Why Nastase feels compelled to cheapen everything he touches is beyond understanding, but I think it must be clear by now that, for a man with his earning power, little wrist slaps like fines of a few thousand dollars or short suspensions mean nothing at all," wrote Wind. "Tennis has rules, and whenever Nastase breaks them he should immediately be defaulted. If he insists on breaking the rules regularly, he should be suspended—for six months or a year, depending on the circumstances. It is as simple as that. Ilie Nastase is an extremely talented athlete, but the success of tennis tournaments assuredly does not depend on whether or not he is appearing."

Not nearly so much concern would be lavished upon Nastase if he were not so magnetic a personality or so skillful a player. But the truth is that tennis has rarely known a performer so smooth, swift, graceful, or technically talented. With a flick of the wrist, particularly on the backhand which is the bugaboo of so many duffers, Nastase can do things others only dream of. Sometimes he seems to be cradling the racquet in only his thumb and forefinger, and with this loose grip he can flick his racquet like a jockey with his riding crop. And when Nasty is on his game, his drop shots and overheads and service and volleys can be devastating. Indeed, in that tournament in Stockholm when he drove wild men wilder in his match with Ashe, he came back to meet hometowner Bjorn Borg in the final and played virtually flawlessly in wiping out the young Swede in straight sets, and allowing him only five games in them.

That tournament, by the way, the Masters Grand Prix, works this way: Tournaments are held around the world from the middle of May to the end of November—forty-eight in 1976 in twenty-two countries. A percentage of the purse is deducted by the sponsors of each tournament and is matched by the Commercial Union Assurance Company, a multinational firm with headquarters in London and a thoroughly organized and lively tennis-promotion office in Boston—that was the situation until 1977 when Colgate took over as principal benefactor. At the end of each year the pooled funds—close to a million dollars—are awarded to the thirty-five leading performers in singles and the twenty best in doubles in each year's Grand Prix tournaments. And Nastase, like most top tennis players, has become a wealthy man in events such as World Championship Tennis and Masters Grand Prix, and is so skilled a performer in them that officials are reluctant to dole out any lasting punishment for his misdeeds. Nasty just goes rolling along, off the court a lovable clown, on it an oaf. He has won the Masters Grand Prix four times, adding this event to his tall triumphs in the U.S. Open, the Canadian Open, and the French and Italian national championships.

"By our American standards," Arthur Ashe has said of him, "he is utterly tactless." Nastase calls Ashe "Negroni," which is Rumanian for black. He calls Stan Smith "Godzilla," disdainful of Smith's size. He calls all South Africans "Racist," as in "Hi Racist, what's up?" Jan Kodes, a Czech who understandably is not enamored of the Soviet Union, is "Russian" to Nastase. His humor can be low humor. One time he partnered Ashe in a tournament in Louisville where Ashe, as a director of the Association of Tennis Professionals, had helped draft bylaws that decreed that both members of doubles teams dress in matching colors. Nastase rushed onto the court to join his partner—in blackface.

"How can you be mad at him for long?" Ashe asked once. "He's a child."

Nastase grew up in a middle-class family in Bucharest where he was born on July 19, 1946, the son of a banker whose home faced onto the Progresul Club where young Ilie and his older brother Constantine could watch tennis by the time they could walk and play it when they were big enough to run. Both did precisely that, too. Constantine was a Rumanian Davis Cup player before Ilie made the team. Ilie was heavily involved in soccer, which is really the national sport of Europe, before he turned seriously to tennis. As a youngster he was always prankish and good humored, beautifully coordinated, and a rising star early. In 1966 when he was twenty, he ended Ion Tiriak's eight-year reign as Rumanian national champion, and by his mid-twenties in the early 1970s he became an international tennis figure. He won the Italian in 1970 and 1973, whipping Spain's clever left-hander Manuel Orantes in the 1973 final with loss of only three games in the three sets. Two weeks later in Paris he didn't drop a set in winning the French Championship. But, really, by then Nasty had already made his indelible mark: In the summer of 1972 he gained the final round at Wimbledon and three months later he won the U.S. crown at Forest Hills.

At Wimbledon that summer Nastase credited the great old Briton Fred Perry, who'd won there in the mid-1930s, with the tip that got him past Orantes in straight sets in the semis and into the final against America's Stan Smith who'd kayoed Jan Kodes in his half of the draw. "Before the tournament began, Fred told me, 'If you can beat yourself, you can win Wimbledon'," Nastase revealed. Fred was wrong. Nasty controlled Nasty in the final, but Smith controlled the final—narrowly. This turned into a five-set thriller in which the two players, each twenty-five years old and each a lieutenant in his own country's armed forces, "made some unbelievable returns," according to United Press International. They also "smashed with venom, hit passing shots on both sides, hit deep and penetrating volleys and hoisted some telling lobs." They went to the fifth set all even. After ten games in it there still was nothing to separate them, although Nastase, showing no inclination to comply with those whose analyses of his psyche is that he chokes, saved two match points in that tenth game to even things at 5–5. Smith held his serve to inch ahead again, and it looked like 6–6 as Nastase sailed away to a 40–0 lead in the twelfth game.

But the raw-boned and lanky Smith, flicking back his straight blond hair with quick little left-hand stabs, whacked a service return for a winner, got a life on Nasty's fifth doublefault of the match, and made deuce on a fine crosscourt backhand. Then he won his fourth straight point and gained his third match point with a driving forehand to Nastase's feet.

Undaunted, Nasty skipped out of danger by punching a forehand volley against the line to deuce things again. Smith gained yet another match point with another sizzling crosscourt forehand out of Nasty's volleying reach and, with the match hanging there, two hours and forty minutes after the start, Nastase dumped a backhand volley into the net and Smith had the deciding set by 7–5.

Nasty's deportment was marvellous; he was a charming loser—but still a loser.

Three months later, things were turned right around. Nasty was a cad. People booed him at Forest Hills. He tossed a towel in the air, grumbling and muttering, and he whacked a ball in the direction of a line official who'd called a couple of shots in the favor of his final-round opponent, Arthur Ashe. There was one other difference: Nasty won.

It was a five-set cliffhanger again, as his match with Stan Smith in Wimbledon's center court had been, but this time Nastase moved into full command after Ashe won a tiebreaker in the third set to go ahead, two sets to one. Mooching around the court like a guy who'd lost three straight photo finishes at the race track, Nastase drove the crowd of 14,696 to a frenzy with his gestures and attitude. But he kept hitting the ball over the net one more time than Ashe. Doing that, he nipped away with the $25,000 top prize by winning the last two sets 6–4, 6–3.

Succeeding years brought peaks and valleys for the gifted and unpredictable Nasty. Typical was his 1976 Wimbledon when he whistled through to the final without loss of a set and then was creamed in straight sets by Bjorn Borg, the man he'd taken apart with loss of only five games in three sets in Stockholm.

He left some observers with the notion he was a sort of Rumanian Holden Caulfield, the wondrous and puzzled young hero of J. D. Salinger's *Catcher in the Rye*. Barry Lorge, writing in *Tennis* magazine in June 1976, was one of these, noting that Nastase was a nonmalicious breaker of rules. "He means well and intends to keep his word every time he promises he's going to shape up," Lorge observed. "But it never seems to work out that way."

The tempestuous Ion Tiriak didn't see his old countryman and teammate in quite that light. "He is scared to lose, he is scared to win, he is scared of everything," growled the bearded and hulking patriarch of Rumanian tennis. "Nastase does not have a brain; he has a bird fluttering around in his head."

Bjorn Borg

BJORN BORG

[1956–   ]

IN ALL THE YEARS since 1920 when the skills of Bill Tilden revolutionized and popularized international tennis,
there was nothing to match a phenomenon at Wimbledon
in 1973 when a seventeen-year-old Swede, Bjorn Borg,
became the idol of every girl old enough to own her own
pimples.

It was as though the Beatles had landed again. Borg's
youth and flowing blond hair and gaunt good looks
turned him into something rarely seen in the staid old
game—a sex symbol. And he remained that for adoles-
cent girls in Britain and Canada and the United States in
succeeding years while his ferocious topspin forehand
was turning him into one of the world's most successful
players.

As Wimbledon approached in that summer of 1973,
anyone who knew of Borg knew of him as a player of the
future. His name was on few fans' lips. What *was* on everyone's lips was word of a player boycott of the Wimbledon tournament over an issue involving Hungarian pro
Nikola Pilic and his country's Davis Cup committee. The
committee appealed to the international federation
which, in turn, induced Wimbledon to turn down Nikki
Pilic's entry, and when that happened almost all of the
world's eminent pros struck the tournament in a power

struggle for recognition. Immediately, Borg became the darling of the media and the hordes of teen-age girls who mobbed him wherever he went. Without the boycott, it's unlikely Borg would have received much ink or television exposure. With it, he and "Borg's Horde" became the top attraction of the early rounds of the tournament.

"I was on my way to a restaurant and I was attacked by about 300 girls," Borg recalled of the phenomenon's birth. "They dragged me down onto the road and I lay there for at least a quarter of an hour without a chance of getting up until the police rescued me. Was I scared? Well, yes, I was a little, as I lay there with the girls all over me. But it was fun, too, to be appreciated. It was all new to me."

Perhaps the young man's appeal would have died right there had he not turned out to be a highly attractive figure on the courts, capturing headlines and attention wherever his world tennis travels took him. He didn't win Wimbledon that summer of 1973 but he did jump into the hearts of the tennis public, especially the younger ones, and by 1974 the titles began to come, too.

That year Borg put together the Italian and French Championships, the youngest player ever to do so, completing the back-to-back feat in Rome and Paris just as he turned eighteen in June. In 1975 he won the French again, and late in the year almost single-handedly carried Sweden to its first Davis Cup championship, a 3–2 squeaker over Czechoslovakia in which, nonetheless, Borg didn't lose a set in two singles matches or in the doubles where he partnered Ove Bengtson.

And in the following year he was even more prominent. Still nineteen, he won the World Championship of

Tennis title, beating Argentina's powerful left-hander
Guillermo Vilas 1–6, 6–1, 7–5, 6–1 in the last round.
WCT, the organization put together in 1968 by Texas
millionaire Lamar Hunt, staged twenty-seven tournaments in twelve countries in 1976, each for a purse of
$60,000, with the eight most successful players qualifying
for the WCT Final in Dallas for another $50,000 winner's
purse. That brought Borg's earnings, before he had
turned twenty, to just under half a million dollars.

A month after his twentieth birthday, Borg topped this
Texas triumph by winning the holy grail at Wimbledon,
toying with heavily favored Ilie Nastase. Neither dropped
a set en route to the final, but Nasty couldn't win one in it
and was dumped by 6–4, 6–2, and 9–7. Thus, the Nordic
nomad became the youngest Wimbledon champion in the
forty-five years since the American Sidney B. Wood won
in 1931, and the first to run through the twelve-day tournament without a loss of a set in the twenty-three years
since another American, Chuck McKinley, did it in
1953.

He did these things with the chilliest of on-court personalities; he was a blond impassive iceberg and full-time
stoic. The Swedes, in general the least expressive and sad-
dest looking of people, have a phrase for this locked-in
look: *is i magen*—ice in the stomach. So partly Borg's facade was inherent—but partly too it was the result of his
veneration of Rod Laver, the player who, as Borg wrote,
"completely masters the art of detaching himself from the
audience and the umpire and who never reveals his in-
nermost feelings; the world's best poker player." Borg
carried a tall admiration for this detachment.

Few players ever assaulted the peaks as quickly as the

lean youngster with the flowing yellow locks. Virtually unknown as Wimbledon began in 1973, he was a world figure by the time he'd won there in 1976. A few months afterwards he just missed ranking as the world's No. 1 player when he was shaded by Jimmy Connors in the Forest Hills final, a remarkable three-year climb.

The match with Connors was one of the year's true highlights. It was, in the words of Herbert Warren Wind in *The New Yorker,* "likely to be assured of a niche in the annals of tennis because its outcome was decided by the most galvanic and fascinating tie-breaker that has been played in a major championship since the tie-breaker made its first appearance in our Open (in 1970) as a means of shortening the boring marathon sets that afflicted tournament tennis."

This was an engagement viewed by millions, internationally televised on a September weekend and matching the world's two best young players, the Wimbledon champion against the *enfant terrible.* Connors had rushed through his half on the draw, seldom in finer form, rarely hitting the ball harder, giving no one a breather. Borg by contrast, had apparently decided the way to play Forest Hill's slow Har-Tru courts was with a sliced and accurate first service, and with infinite patience from the baseline once the ball was in play. If his opponents went to the net on him, Borg's style was to use looping topspin lifts off his two-handed backhand or fiery slashes with the forehand to pass and discourage them.

This style had been effective, though dicey and painstaking, in the early stages. For instance, Brian Gottfried won two sets and led 2–0 in the third before Borg finally got to him and sneaked past in five sets. Next, defending champion Manuel Orantes, who endured a shaky 1976, got his game going against Borg and was another nip-and-tuck five-set victim. Borg, obviously, was in wonderful physical condition, able to run for hours and prepared to chase down any ball that crossed to his side of the net.

The final, then, was a sensational match from the beginning when Connors indicated his game plan: he'd simply hit everything he could reach with everything he had. And, on this particular day, the balls he was hitting with absolutely blazing speed were clipping the tapes. He was hitting his two-handed backhand so hard much of the time that his swing actually was lifting both his feet off the court.

But in spite of this power, he was not blowing Borg out of the stadium. Anticipating grandly, fighting for everything, hammering back whatever he could lay his racquet on, the Swede hung in. He was beaten narrowly at 6–4 in the first set, and when Connors let down a little in the second set Borg quickly jumped into the opening, breaking Connors at love to go ahead 4–2 and holding twice to win, 6–3.

Connors seemed to have the third tucked away, leading 4–2 and 40–love and then had another brief lapse, dropped five points in a row, yielded Borg's serve, and that tied the set at 4–4. When they got to 6–6 there began the magnetic tiebreaker, an affair that had people shouting at their television screens in their homes. In this seven-point overtime it turned out that twenty points were needed before a winner was known, and in the spine-tingling session Borg held set point four times and Connors twice in marvellous seesaw exchanges.

Borg led at 6–4, needing only a point to wrap up the game and the set. Connors tied it at 6–6, then went ahead 7–6 and *he* needed only one point to win. Borg tied it, went ahead at 8–7 and for the third time required only the next point for victory. But Connors tied it at 8–8. Borg went ahead 9–8 for his fourth set point and again Connors fought him off, tied it, went ahead 10–9 and, with *his* second set point facing him, he brought it off for an 11–9 win. This decided not just the third set but the match as well because the disappointed Borg, who had been so near so often, could not get his heart truly into the fourth set and Connors wrapped it up at 6–4.

Still, it was a marvellous year for the young man just three months past twenty, and it was with a feeling of high accomplishment that he and his parents returned to the mansion he'd bought in Monte Carlo. This home was the result of his influx of money that with his many endorsements—comic books, cupcakes, breakfast cereal, blue jeans, a headband that advertised a beer, a patch on his shirt that promoted the Swedish air line, SAS—reached close to a million dollars in 1976. The huge income induced him to relocate himself and his parents on the French Rivera to avoid the large taxes of socialist Sweden. It set up the unusual situation of the young athlete being a hero of a country he scarcely even visits. "There is nothing I miss about Sweden except the people," Borg has said.

His parents are Marguerite and Rune Borg, people of widely disparate personalities, each of whom has been cast in the blond money machine with the ferocious forehand. Marguerite is fair-haired, outgoing, and garrulous. Rune is brown-haired, stares impassively, and says little.

She is Bjorn's seldom-seen lighter side; he is the on-the-court stoic. They are medium-sized, unpretentious, and when they travel the world with him they usually dress casually in rumpled beige suede, watching his matches with no outward show of emotion, rarely a change of expression. Sweden is filled with sphinxes; you see them on the streets of Stockholm, magnificently attractive women with their somber faces, and on the subways, staring lugubriously into space. Borg's parents are the faces of Sweden transported to the courtsides of the world.

Hating the winters, Borg often takes time off from tournaments in the northern hemisphere during winter to fly himself and his parents to some exotic island in the South Pacific or the West Indies. Then he returns to the ice-encrusted tennis circuit, fresh and invigorated. It is at these times that the mask the tennis fans see on the courts will come off in the locker rooms, revealing a real live boy with a merry twinkle in the light blue eyes. He'll produce a jovial spirit sometimes in explaining a dark, sparse, scraggly accumulation of hair along his jaw, a dreadful excuse for a beard.

"No, no, not a beard!" he'll exclaim, laughing in small embarrassment. "I have these sun blisters from last week when my parents and I go to Puerto Rico. We are not used to the strong sun, being from Sweden. I cannot take away the whiskers until they heal." He'll gingerly touch a mouth ringed in small scabs and tiny blisters. He grins again when it is suggested to him that these are small prices to pay for the life he leads. He pulls a knee-length raccoon coat over faded jeans and cotton T-shirt, hikes the collar's fur high against his tumbled hair, and prepares to make a run through the teeming groupies who keep squirming, gum-snapping, restless vigil outside the locker room. His parents are beyond the door, beyond the milling girls, and Marguerite Borg is entertained by the darting-eyed groupies, an unknown phenomenon in Stockholm and Monte Carlo. "In Stockholm, everyone knows Bjorn, they're used to him," she laughs. "In Monte Carlo, there are so many famous people he is not bothered. In England and America, though, there are many of these." There's no rancor; she doesn't mind that the glassy-eyed kids are waiting to squeal at her Bjorn. She's amused, watching them. If Rune feels any emotion, he masks it. His eyes are unblinking behind brown hornrims.

The object of all this commotion was born on June 6, 1956, the only child of Marguerite and Rune, who were grocery keepers. He grew up in Sodertalje, a small town near Stockholm, where hockey was his consuming interest until he was nine. Then, his father came home with a tennis racquet, a prize he won in a Ping-Pong tournament, and it was at that moment, as flippant journalists were later to write, that a star was Bjorn.

"Like most small boys in Sodertalje, I had idols on the hockey team," he wrote in his autobiography. "My great aim was to become a national hockey player with the Sodertalje Sports Club." When his father brought home the tennis racquet, though, Bjorn reached what he likes to call the turning point in his life. "I played imaginary matches against the garage wall. I invented international matches between Sweden and the USA. If I managed to keep the ball in play a certain number of times, Sweden won the point. If I missed, the USA did." By the time he was twelve, he was winning medals. By fourteen, he had dropped hockey. By fifteen, he had even dropped school. He was so completely wrapped up in hockey that he never completed grade nine.

"I know that this decision came as a sensation to many people," he wrote. "But my parents and I considered there was no alternative. I knew my marks would get worse and worse because I used all my time playing tennis. So it would be quite meaningless simply to go on sitting there between 8 A.M. and 3 P.M., wasting my time." On the grounds that he had already picked a profession, he was given permission to leave school. He was fifteen.

By then he had been working for five years with a coach, Percy Rosberg, an instructor the Swedish Tennis Association had sent to Sodertalje to train the leading juniors. In those five years young Borg reached a level of play that earned him a place on Sweden's Davis Cup team, which is not something to be confused, of course, with gaining a similar spot on Australia's or the U.S.'s— Sweden, to be sure, was not quite a world tennis power. Nonetheless, Borg was one of the youngest players in all David Cup history, shaded only by Haroon Rahim of Pakistan, who was thirteen months younger than Borg's fifteen when the latter engaged New Zealand's No. 1 player, Onny Parun, in May 1972.

In this match, Borg established a pattern that was to become familiar to people following his career: he blew the first two sets and came back to win three in a row. "I have never been troubled by nerves, and I really am just as calm as I look," Borg's autobiography says. Some of the world's great players learned the truth of Borg's words in the years that followed; poor Parun didn't know that then, of course, and was desolated in his 4–6, 3–6,

6–3, 6–4, 6–4 loss to this unknown Swede of a mere fifteen with not a visible nerve in his makeup. "Stubbornness
is my strength," Borg wrote. "Persistence is my strongest
point. I never give up in a match, however down I am. In
this respect, tennis is a fantastic game. You can be hope-
lessly down, as long as you win the last point."

By 1974 Borg had become the youngest player ever to
win a major championship, taking the Italian in May and
adding the French in June. In 1975 he won a second
French and over the course of the year led his country to
a Davis Cup triumph that up to then he regarded as his
finest victory ever and one the country's newspapers
heralded as the greatest Swedish sports achievement since
Ingemar Johansson won the world's heavyweight boxing
championship in 1959 by knocking out Floyd Patterson.
It turned Sweden into the first European country in more
than forty years to win the Davis Cup, and only the seventh country to win it since the competition was inaugu-
rated in 1900. In the opening singles Borg whipped Jiri
Hrebec, 6–1, 6–3, 6–0, then teamed with Bengtson to beat
Vladimir Zednik and Jan Kodes, 6–4, 6–4, 6–4. In the
match that settled the issue, young Borg handled the
fiery Kodes by 6–4, 6–2, 6–2, beating the former Wimbledon champion in just under two hours. "I finally made it
in a match like this, which I think surpasses anything else
in world tennis," Borg exulted in uncharacteristic enthusiasm. "I've never been so nervous before a big match. I
could only sleep four or five hours in the night."

Borg was beaten fortuitously six months later in the
quarterfinals of the French Championship at Stade Roland Garros. He was beaten by the handsome and
smooth-swinging Italian, Adriano Panatta, who had won

his own country's national championship in Rome and went on to win the French in Paris. This was a favorable loss for Borg because it gave him nearly a week's rest plus another week to spend up to five hours a day with his mentor Lennert Bergelin developing a big serve and volley game on grass for Wimbledon.

Until that summer of 1976 most of Borg's victories were a result of his patience, his persistence, his physical condition, and his determination on comparatively slow clay. Now, with Bergelin's attendance, Borg got ready for the lightning-like qualities of grass in daily workouts at the Cumberland Club in North London.

When he arrived at Wimbledon he treated spectators to a Borg they'd rarely if ever seen in action. The ball simply darted off his tightly strung racquet from the service line, and when he reached the semifinals against the cannonball services of Roscoe Tanner he was rifling shots every bit as swift as the American left-hander's. Tanner, it was felt, would do well against Borg, perhaps even beat him, because, as the conqueror of pre-tournament favorite Jimmy Connors, he was at the very peak of his game. Instead, Borg scarcely took a deep breath with him, and disposed of him in straight sets at 6–4, 9–8 in a tie-breaker, and 6–4.

Borg had not dropped a set in reaching the final, though from the fourth round on his future had been in jeopardy because he had pulled a stomach muscle, no doubt in his strenuous preparations for Wimbledon and in the vastly greater effort he was putting into his serves in the tournament itself. He took cortisone injections before he went out onto the court each day, and occasionally during matches he used an anesthetic spray to control the pain. He did this in the final as well, where he was opposed by the colorful and controversial screwball Nastase, who also had not dropped a set in route to the final. In the early moments, old Nasty appeared headed for another lustrous day in the stifling and unusual heat and humidity that assailed Wimbledon all through its twelve days of 1976.

Nastase won the first three games and was ahead 40–0 with Borg serving in the fourth. But then the indomitable Swede served like a demon, fought furiously on the three break points, and brought the score to deuce. Then he ran out the game in what, so early in the match, turned out to be its turning point. Had Nastase got ahead 4–0, things might have been different. Down only 1–3 instead, Borg broke Nastase and then won himself to tie it at 3–3, and Nastase never really had a look after that. He was beaten 6–4, 6–2, and 9–7 in precisely 107 minutes before a royal assemblage that included the King and Queen of Greece, the Queen Mother of Denmark, the Duke and Duchess of Kent, the Rumanian and Swedish Ambassadors to Britain, the Lord Mayor of London, assorted generals and admirals, and more than 14,000 people, some of whom had lined up in the intense heat for fifty hours and others who had paid the equivalent of $180 for a pair of tickets. For Bjorn Borg, it was a very long way from the meaninglessness of sitting in a grade nine classroom from 8 A.M. to 3 P.M. in a little town called Sodertalje—something on the order of a million miles from the center court at Wimbledon.

JIMMY CONNORS

[1952–   ]

THERE WERE QUESTIONS for tennis watchers after twenty-four-year-old Jimmy Connors won the U.S. national championship for the second time in three years in September 1976. Did this tall triumph achieved in a searing final with Bjorn Borg mark the end of the longest adolescence in tennis history? Was Connors twenty-four going on twenty-five or was he twenty-four going on, as usual, fifteen? In short, had the young man with the indisputable talent and the Prince Valiant hairdo finally matured, or was this talent permanently joined with a thoroughly disconcerting personality?

In the years leading up to his second win in the horse-shoe bowl at Forest Hills, Connors had managed to disenchant most people who follow tennis. His immaturity had manifested itself on almost as many courts as his truly devastating tennis game—and that took in a lot of courts in a lot of countries. For by the time Connors reached twenty-two years on the calendar he had won the national titles of the United States, Italy, and Australia and had scored convincingly (indeed, overwhelmingly, in a terrifying rout of the popular veteran Ken Rosewall) in the final round at Wimbledon. Chances are he'd have added the French Championship to his list in 1974, giving him a

Jimmy Connors

Grand Slam sweep, but tennis politics made him ineligible for the French that year.

For obscure reasons, his on-court deportment included an apparent determination to be a gamesman, an entertainer, and a comic, but all he really succeeded in being in the opinion of most people was a jerk. For instance, after an opponent had made a particularly good shot, it was often Connors' custom to place his right hand inside his shirt and wigwag it vigorously over his heart to demonstrate how frightened the shot had made him. This self-indulgence, and other similar juvenile antics, usually were accompanied by a smirk.

Connors' attempts at humor during matches he had well in hand ranged from childish to obscene, his exaggerated mincing strides were embarrassing, and many of his swaggering routines left audiences in uncomfortable silence. The pity was that he apparently couldn't sense the negative reaction his posturings induced in people; he thought he was a cut-up—or, at any rate, that's what his demeanor suggested. "He thinks he's Bob Hope," the Australian Phil Dent said once, "but he's about as funny as bloody Marcus Welby."

However, there were indications that with the 1976 Forest Hills victory over Borg in one of the great national finals, Connors had finally grown past pablum and was ready for filet mignon. Through the two weeks of the tournament he was unfailingly courteous with the press, all the officials, the little old ladies, and even the squirming kids jamming for autographs. In a quite startling about-face, Connors dispensed with the gauche image. And, on the court he appeared committed to vindicating himself for a lackluster 1975 when he often had to settle for second-place prize money. This, in turn, was in contrast to 1974 when he looked like the dominating force for the 1970s that Rod Laver had been in the previous decade.

In the match with Borg everything came together for him again. He was as dedicated as a hungry middleweight, injecting loud harsh grunts into every serve and many a two-fisted backhand screamer, smashing low line drives crosscourt and down the lines like a guy using a rifle, and in the end emerging by 6–4, 3–6, 7–6, 6–4. As Herbert Warren Wind, the fastidious onlooker from *The New Yorker,* was to observe, "his conquest of Borg stands, in a way, as the finest victory of his career. In many ways, Jimmy Connors still hasn't grown up, but this triumph, which he wanted so badly, could be of inestimable value."

Connors began hitting the magazine covers regularly in 1974 when he won with ease at Wimbledon and Forest Hills and then buried Rod Laver in a televised extravaganza at Las Vegas. He followed up these successes early in 1975 by knocking off the popular Aussie John Newcombe in another of the Nevada excesses. These head-to-head matchups involved so much money that the numbers grew meaningless, and they established Connors, at twenty-two, as the world's highest paid tennis player. His skill at rifling perfect shots from anywhere on the court left people who had spent a lifetime in the game shaking their heads in near disbelief. Far less admirable was his curious talent for alienating audiences—shouting vulgarities, smirking, mincing, middle-fingering linesmen who blew a call or fans who jibed him, and stalling when an opponent got ahead.

Connors is the product of what used to be called a

stage mother, except that his mother Gloria and *her* mother, Bertha Thompson, both of them one-time teaching professionals, picked the tennis court rather than the Broadway stage for the little boy's platform. As a child of two, Jimmy began dragging a full-sized tennis racquet in his wake.

"That's how I learned to hit two-handers," he recalled once. "I had to use both my hands to pick up the damn racquet." Gloria and Bertha made sure he picked up only good habits when he picked up the bat, and Connors never has forgotten or misplaced this debt to his mother. "She could have been a touring pro, but instead she decided to devote full time to me," he said. "That's how I got here."

Jimmy's father, James Sr., was manager of a toll bridge connecting East St. Louis, Illinois, where Jimmy was born, and St. Louis, Missouri. He hung in the background, and let his wife have her way with Jimmy's upbringing. Watching the boy grow, he observed that Jimmy's peers resented him then even as they were to later. "He wasn't one of the kids," James recalled. "He was too competitive." James died early in 1977.

By the time Jimmy was five he and an older brother Johnny were deeply immersed in tennis. Tennis was all he wanted to do and even as a child he claims he "never had time for friends or anything else. I didn't even know anybody in school. I was too busy. I used to leave class every day at noon to practice tennis." There, he developed one of his major skills, his ability to return service, *any* service, for winners, by working out on the hardwood floor of an armory, the world's fastest surface. It forced him to challenge every serve early, utilizing his opponent's speed, taking the ball on the rise before it could handcuff him. He never lost this extraordinary ability to turn an opponent's cannonballs to his own advantage.

Earlier, though, when he was five and playing against older brother Johnny, their heated confrontations on an asphalt court in the front yard of their home were so strenuous that they often drew crowds. Two little kids, fierce as cock fighters. "Tennis was everything to them," James Connors reflected once, "my wife, her mother, the boys, they were all into it. Whether it was Christmas, New Year's or birthdays, there was always some tournament to enter."

Being older, Johnny had the physical assets to appear more promising. But winning became an obsession with Jimmy who, as his late father noted, "had an added spark." The spark or the obsession drove Johnny out of competitive tennis by the time he was twelve. Mother Gloria had no regrets. "Johnny just didn't have the guts for competitive tennis," was the way she phrased it. Meantime, she and Bertha, whom Jimmy called Two-Mom, kept working on the lad's fundamental strokes and his approach to the game (though apparently giving short shrift to his deportment) and when he was sixteen decided he'd learned everything he could about tennis from them. So the three of them packed their bags and went to California and looked up Pancho Segura, a gnarled and weathered and skilled pro whom Gloria had known in her tennis days twenty years earlier. Segura and another Pancho, the one-time lion of tennis, Gonzales, took on the polishing of young Connors' game at the Beverly Hills Tennis Club. Gloria kept the family eating by teaching tennis. She must have done well as an instructor, for she bought a car for Jimmy. The youngster managed to graduate from high school while spending most of his time on the court, and learning about clothes and girls from Spencer Segura, Pancho's teen-age son, and Dino Martin, the singer's son.

In 1971 Jimmy enrolled at UCLA and as a freshman won the National Collegiate Athletic Association's tennis championship before dropping out of school after one semester. No one really knows why he bothered to drop into UCLA at all, unless it was to qualify for the NCAA tournament. He left school in January 1972 to become a peripatetic professional, and in due course a rich one, with the wily Segura encouraging his counter-punching style, his quickness, and his aggressiveness. Also guiding him was a flamboyant, red-faced manager, Bill Riordan, who ran a small pro circuit and whose style and manner had made an impression on Two-Mom Bertha. She recommended him to handle Jimmy's off-court business. Connors passed up the richer-by-far World Championship Tennis circuit to join Riordan's. "I felt it was better for my confidence to play there in the beginning," he rationalized. "In the WCT I probably would have lost a lot of first round matches."

At that stage, though, no one was paying much attention to Connors, and didn't until 1972's Wimbledon when he showed up on the arm of the new darling of the media, calm and contained Chris Evert, the Floridian star of women's tennis. He was overshadowed by her on and off the court, and although he won a tournament here and there he never got further than the quarterfinals in

183

any of the big national events. That year he won seven tournaments and about $90,000 in prize money, and was ranked No. 3 in the U.S.

In the summer of 1973, though, his game began to come together and he won the U.S. Pro championship against top competition, beating Arthur Ashe in the final in a five-setter. Then he hopped continents to Johannesburg where he beat Ashe again in the South Africa final. But he had major losses, too. Alex Metreveli eliminated him early at Wimbledon, John Newcombe shelved him in straight sets at Forest Hills, and in December at the Grand Prix Masters windup he was hammered for the ninth time in ten meetings with Ilie Nastase. Still, he was co-ranked No. 1 in America with Stan Smith by the USLTA, partly because Smith was skidding from the heights. It had been anything but a bad year for Connors; along with his shared ranking as the country's top player he won $130,000 and became engaged to Chrissie, either of which rated well above a double fault on match point.

Connors went to Australia and won the national championship there in January 1974, then returned to the modest Bill Riordan circuit in the U.S., confounding most fans who wanted to see him against the top performers in the WCT. Riordan had been a boxing promoter and men's wear salesman who became director of the USLTA's indoor tennis circuit. In 1973 that circuit was cut back to make way for the WCT and Riordan was dismissed. He insisted that he be allowed to stay in business at least as an independent promoter managing what was left of the association's old indoor circuit, and the board agreed.

When Connors joined that group he got the experience he needed, and as he became a tougher player Riordan suddenly found himself with the hottest property in tennis, especially after Connors made mincemeat out of little Ken (Muscles) Rosewall in the Wimbledon final. Spectators literally were shielding their eyes from the center court fiasco as Connors whistled to a 6–1, 6–1, 6–4 victory. The situation was even worse, astonishingly enough, three months later at Forest Hills. There, Connors and Rosewall met again in the final, and this time strong men wept as Connors simply humiliated the Aussie veteran, administering the worst defeat ever inflicted on anyone in the final round of the tournament. Scores were 6–1, 6–0, 6–1 in a match of a mere sixty-nine minutes. Rosewall won only nineteen points in the three sets, and winning such a match from such a legend by such a score did nothing for Connors' image with tennis fans.

At one point in the second set a voice halfway up the concrete horseshoe bellowed like an Ebbets Field voice from the past, "You're a bum, Connors!"

To his credit, Jimmy smiled and waved his racquet in a sort of salute to the voice. "I agree," he muttered in what seemed a serious vein.

Later, in the press tent, Connors was to reflect on the shocking one-sided nature of the match: "I've seen people pity Ken Rosewall and then see him win 6–3 in the fifth. In the back of my mind I held the thought that if I let down Rosewall could win it. I was afraid I'd come down. I had to keep the pressure on."

The predicament of Connors by the end of 1974 was surely unprecedented for a champion. Fans were upset with him, his fellow pros were down on him, and the press was usually snide with him, although each of these groups was prepared to concede that he was the world's No. 1 player. Most galleries resented his lack of manners, the press had never been able to warm up to his undiluted brassiness, and fellow pros resented him because, as Arthur Ashe had observed even as Connors was emerging in the top echelon in 1973, "they think he goes a little heavy on the gamesmanship—the hand-blowing and the ball-bouncing before he serves is just a little too studied." But the major resentment was his refusal to join the players' union, ATP, the Association of Tennis Players. As Ashe noted, "It is galling when somebody like Connors comes along and benefits without doing his part."

Connors apparently didn't think he'd benefitted all that much. When he was ineligible for the French Open in 1974 and thereby missed a shot at the Grand Slam he hit the directors of ATP with a $41 million lawsuit "by allegedly conspiring with organizers of the French Open" to bar him and others from the tournament because they weren't playing the European summer circuit.

And, finally, almost everyone was dismayed when Connors, apparently on the advice of manager Riordan, refused to play on the Davis Cup team for his country, claiming it was selected and managed unfairly. Further, he wouldn't play for a team captained by Dennis Ralston. Without Connors, the American team was an embarrassing early-round victim, first of Colombia and then Mexico in successive years.

Out of all of this, the best player in tennis emerged as a mop-haired, immature creation of a stage mother and a protective manager, the least liked star in sports, five feet ten inches of unadorned controversy. That, anyway, is the way Pete Axthelm, the *Newsweek* sports editor, viewed him in a major piece in early 1975. "After victories at Wimbledon and Forest Hills and total winnings of $286,000 last year, Connors has the credentials and the ego to handle any role that his promotion people dream up for him," Axthelm wrote. "Yelling and gesturing at his hecklers and slashing brilliant shots past his opponents, he has found fun and profit in being the man they love to hate."

But Axthelm saw more than the superficial figure, and concluded there was more to Connors than his mawkish image. "When he relaxes around a few beers and a stack of rock 'n' roll oldies with California friends like Dino Martin Jr. and Pancho Segura's son Spencer, Jimmy's humor becomes less strained and his on-court meanness softens. And behind his brash, ill-at-ease victory speeches, he often displays surprising humility and emotion. The day after his victory at Wimbledon, for example, he confided to a friend, 'People would never believe it about me but I almost started to cry yesterday. I looked over at my mother and thought of how hard she and I had worked to get here. Then I looked at Ken Rosewall, a guy I grew up reading about. Now I'm twenty-two and I've beaten him and won something that he never won. I was really shook.' "

Connors turned 1975 into a conundrum by losing his fiancée and his titles, winning enormous amounts of money, and remaining firmly in the public eye, his image intact. He won hundreds of thousands of dollars by beating first Rod Laver and then John Newcombe a few months apart at Las Vegas in television spectaculars to rival heavyweight championship fights in their promotional pizazz and hype. Yet he lost all his major titles though sweeping to the final in each and appearing, until each unexpected defeat, to be tearing the tournament to shreds. Newcombe laced him in a thrilling finale to the Australian Open by 7–5, 3–6, 6–4, and 7–6, the last-set tiebreaker being an exciting thing won by Newk at nine points to seven, with Connors only a point away from the victory at 7–6.

There followed the Connors defeat at Wimbledon where the exhaustively—but not exhaustedly—prepared Arthur Ashe scored an enormous upset by sticking to a game plan by which he threw mostly junk at Connors, depriving Jimmy of his counterpunching prowess, and giving him drop shots and chips and lobs. The 11–2 underdog won in four sets by 6–1, 6–1, 5–7, and 6–4.

And then came Forest Hills where the grass had gone the way of, well, of Ebbets Field—it had simply disappeared, a hallowed tradition evicted like an impoverished tenant. Clay-like surface called Har-Tru replaced the grass at Forest Hills just as faceless highrises had replaced Ebbets Field but, in spite of this, the smash, hammer, crash of Connors' game that is so effective on grass was quite as devastating on the slower stuff, and he whistled through the early rounds. But then he was opposed by the gracious Spaniard Manuel Orantes in the final. Orantes provided an unexpected climax to a marvellous tournament for his left-handed thrusts by handling all the fire-power Connors could direct at him and scoring yet another upset over a favorite now deprived of all his major titles, as well as the hand of the country's major woman's tennis talent, Chris Evert. The love match made in heaven, or right near there, ended when she returned the South African diamond engagement ring to Jimmy. The Lovebird Double had gone *phffft*.

In 1976 almost everything else in Connors' life underwent a turnaround if not exactly a *phffft*. He dropped all the lawsuits. He forsook Bill Riordan's modest tennis caravan and joined the big boys in the WCT. He even forsook Bill Riordan, and his mom Gloria took on the manager's duties. He made peace with the Davis Cup team, losing a taut exciting five-setter to Raul Ramirez as Mexico shaded the U.S. in the 1976 eliminations. He departed early at Wimbledon, too.

But there were a lot of pluses. For instance, he lost only seven matches all year—and won an even dozen tournaments. None of these compared, of course, with his September conquest of Borg at Forest Hills. Beating Borg was important, but what most onlookers hoped was that he'd also beaten the brat in Jimmy Connors. To a pulp.

INDEX